# Egypt

# Other Books of Related Interest

## Opposing Viewpoints Series

Afghanistan

The Palestinian Territories

Syria

US Foreign Policy

## At Issue Series

Biological and Chemical Weapons

Does the World Hate the US?

Drones

Is Foreign Aid Necessary?

## Current Controversies Series

Immigration

Pakistan

Politics and Religion

Racial Profiling

# "Congress shall make no law . . . abridging the freedom of speech, or of the press."

*First Amendment to the US Constitution*

The basic foundation of our democracy is the First Amendment guarantee of freedom of expression. The Opposing Viewpoints series is dedicated to the concept of this basic freedom and the idea that it is more important to practice it than to enshrine it.

# OPPOSING VIEWPOINTS® SERIES

# Egypt

*Margaret Haerens, Book Editor*

**GREENHAVEN PRESS**
*A part of Gale, Cengage Learning*

GALE
CENGAGE Learning·

Farmington Hills, Mich • San Francisco • New York • Waterville, Maine
Meriden, Conn • Mason, Ohio • Chicago

Patricia Coryell, *Vice President & Publisher, New Products & GVRL*
Douglas Dentino, *Manager, New Products*
Judy Galens, *Acquisitions Editor*

*For more information, contact:*
Greenhaven Press
27500 Drake Rd.
Farmington Hills, MI 48331-3535
Or you can visit our Internet site at gale.cengage.com

For product information and technology assistance, contact us at

Gale Customer Support, 1-800-877-4253
For permission to use material from this text or product, submit all requests online at www.cengage.com/permissions

Further permissions questions can be emailed to permissionrequest@cengage.com

Articles in Greenhaven Press anthologies are often edited for length to meet page requirements. In addition, original titles of these works are changed to clearly present the main thesis and to explicitly indicate the author's opinion. Every effort is made to ensure that Greenhaven Press accurately reflects the original intent of the authors. Every effort has been made to trace the owners of copyrighted material.

Cover Image copyright © Pakhnyushcha/Shutterstock.com.

**LIBRARY OF CONGRESS CATALOGING-IN-PUBLICATION DATA**

Egypt (2015) Egypt / Margaret Haerens, Book Editor.
    pages cm. -- (Opposing viewpoints)
    Includes bibliographical references and index.
    ISBN 978-0-7377-7256-2 (hardcover) -- ISBN 978-0-7377-7257-9 (pbk.)
    1. Egypt--Politics and government--21st century. 2. Democratization--Egypt.
3. Egypt--History--Protests, 2011- 4. United States--Foreign relations--Egypt.
5. Egypt--Foreign relations--United States. I. Haerens, Margaret, editor of compilation. II. Title. III. Series: Opposing viewpoints series (Unnumbered)
    DT107.88.E34 2015
    962.05'6--dc23
                                                                2014030221

Printed in the United States of America
    1 2 3 4 5        19 18 17 16 15

# Contents

## Chapter 4: What Should Be US Policy on Egypt?

# Why Consider Opposing Viewpoints?

> *"The only way in which a human being can make some approach to knowing the whole of a subject is by hearing what can be said about it by persons of every variety of opinion and studying all modes in which it can be looked at by every character of mind. No wise man ever acquired his wisdom in any mode but this."*
>
> *John Stuart Mill*

In our media-intensive culture it is not difficult to find differing opinions. Thousands of newspapers and magazines and dozens of radio and television talk shows resound with differing points of view. The difficulty lies in deciding which opinion to agree with and which "experts" seem the most credible. The more inundated we become with differing opinions and claims, the more essential it is to hone critical reading and thinking skills to evaluate these ideas. Opposing Viewpoints books address this problem directly by presenting stimulating debates that can be used to enhance and teach these skills. The varied opinions contained in each book examine many different aspects of a single issue. While examining these conveniently edited opposing views, readers can develop critical thinking skills such as the ability to compare and contrast authors' credibility, facts, argumentation styles, use of persuasive techniques, and other stylistic tools. In short, the Opposing Viewpoints Series is an ideal way to attain the higher-level thinking and reading skills so essential in a culture of diverse and contradictory opinions.

In addition to providing a tool for critical thinking, Opposing Viewpoints books challenge readers to question their own strongly held opinions and assumptions. Most people form their opinions on the basis of upbringing, peer pressure, and personal, cultural, or professional bias. By reading carefully balanced opposing views, readers must directly confront new ideas as well as the opinions of those with whom they disagree. This is not to argue simplistically that everyone who reads opposing views will—or should—change his or her opinion. Instead, the series enhances readers' understanding of their own views by encouraging confrontation with opposing ideas. Careful examination of others' views can lead to the readers' understanding of the logical inconsistencies in their own opinions, perspective on why they hold an opinion, and the consideration of the possibility that their opinion requires further evaluation.

## Evaluating Other Opinions

To ensure that this type of examination occurs, Opposing Viewpoints books present all types of opinions. Prominent spokespeople on different sides of each issue as well as well-known professionals from many disciplines challenge the reader. An additional goal of the series is to provide a forum for other, less known, or even unpopular viewpoints. The opinion of an ordinary person who has had to make the decision to cut off life support from a terminally ill relative, for example, may be just as valuable and provide just as much insight as a medical ethicist's professional opinion. The editors have two additional purposes in including these less known views. One, the editors encourage readers to respect others' opinions—even when not enhanced by professional credibility. It is only by reading or listening to and objectively evaluating others' ideas that one can determine whether they are worthy of consideration. Two, the inclusion of such viewpoints encourages the important critical thinking skill of objectively evaluating an author's credentials and bias. This evaluation will illuminate an author's reasons for taking a particular stance on an issue and will aid in readers' evaluation of the author's ideas.

It is our hope that these books will give readers a deeper understanding of the issues debated and an appreciation of the complexity of even seemingly simple issues when good and honest people disagree. This awareness is particularly important in a democratic society such as ours in which people enter into public debate to determine the common good. Those with whom one disagrees should not be regarded as enemies but rather as people whose views deserve careful examination and may shed light on one's own.

Thomas Jefferson once said that "difference of opinion leads to inquiry, and inquiry to truth." Jefferson, a broadly educated man, argued that "if a nation expects to be ignorant and free . . . it expects what never was and never will be." As individuals and as a nation, it is imperative that we consider the opinions of others and examine them with skill and discernment. The Opposing Viewpoints series is intended to help readers achieve this goal.

*David L. Bender and Bruno Leone,*
*Founders*

# Introduction

> *"We, Egyptians, have an extremely diffi-*
> *cult task and a costly mission. The eco-*
> *nomic, social, political, and security re-*
> *alities ... have reached the limit that*
> *requires an honest and brave confronta-*
> *tion of challenges."*
>
> *—General Abdel Fattah al-Sisi,*
> *speech, March 26, 2014*

In late May of 2014, Egypt held a presidential election to determine the country's next leader. It featured only two candidates: the former military general Abdel Fattah al-Sisi and political activist and government opposition leader Hamdeen Sabahi. When the results were announced, the outcome was hardly a surprise. Sisi was overwhelmingly elected on a wave of popular support. Political analysts attributed the electoral rout to his key leadership role in deposing the last democratically elected president, Mohamed Morsi, and his reputation as a tough, competent figure in a time of political and economic instability. Others pointed to Sisi's squashing of political dissent and the persecution of many of his political opponents.

After Sisi's victory was announced, hundreds of thousands of supporters gathered to celebrate in Tahrir Square, a public area in Cairo that had been the location of massive public protests that had brought down the last two Egyptian presidents. Fireworks erupted overhead as the jubilant crowd danced, sang, and chanted. Sisi's election signaled a new era in Egypt and, as many in Tahrir Square that night hoped, an end to much of the violence, civil unrest, political uncertainty, and economic malaise that had characterized the past several years.

In his inauguration speech on June 8, 2014, Sisi vowed to be a leader to all Egyptians but rejected reconciliation with Islamist groups. In a later televised speech, he clearly reiterated this view and called reconciliation with those who "adopted violence as a methodology" as appeasement. "There is no place for them in this march forward," he said in his remarks. "I say it loud and clear: no cooperation or appeasement for those who resort to violence and those who want to disrupt our movement to the future."

Observers suggest that Sisi was referring to the Muslim Brotherhood, the influential Islamist group that had been banned in Egypt since 2013. After the ouster of former Egyptian president Hosni Mubarak on January 25, 2011, by military forces led by General al-Sisi, the Muslim Brotherhood had won the majority of seats in subsequent parliamentary elections. Morsi, a leader of the Muslim Brotherhood and its candidate in the June 2012 presidential election, was elected president by receiving more than 50 percent of the vote.

Once he took office, Morsi squandered the public's trust by granting himself near absolute powers and replacing many trusted officials with allies from the Muslim Brotherhood and other Islamist groups. Reports of attacks on religious minorities became common. Civil liberties were curtailed, and journalists and protesters were beaten by pro-Morsi supporters in the streets. Many Egyptians grew alarmed that Morsi was beginning to impose an Islamist system on the country, based on conservative Islamic law. That view was reinforced when the draft of a new constitution was formulated by Islamic lawmakers that reflected an increasingly rigid Islamism.

Widespread protests and public outrage led to Morsi backtracking on some of his controversial moves, but the damage had been done. On July 3, 2013, he was removed from office by the military, arrested, and replaced by an interim leader. His party, the Muslim Brotherhood, was later banned, and many of its leaders and supporters imprisoned and charged with crimes ranging from inciting violence to espionage.

Sisi's inauguration speech dashed the hopes of many Egyptians that there would be a national reconciliation between the Muslim Brotherhood forces and Sisi supporters, and that it would lead to an inclusive political process and a cessation of political repression against Islamists in Egypt. His words raised concerns that by continuing to bar Islamist groups such as the Muslim Brotherhood from the political process, it would be impossible to bring political, economic, and social stability to Egypt.

The global reaction to Sisi's victory and inauguration was mixed. The United States released a statement after the election, congratulating him and expressing anticipation to working with him on strategic issues in the future. The statement also expressed concern over reports referring to the repressive political atmosphere in the run-up to the election, including the harassment, beating, and imprisonment of political protesters and Morsi supporters. "We have consistently expressed our concerns about limits on freedom of peaceful assembly, association, and expression and call on the government to ensure these freedoms as well as due process rights for all Egyptians," the White House stated.

The White House statement went on to say, "While elections are an integral component of a democratic society, true democracy is built on a foundation of rule of law, civil liberties, and open political discourse. We urge the president-elect and the government to adopt the reforms that are needed to govern with accountability and transparency, ensure justice for every individual, and demonstrate a commitment to the protection of the universal rights of all Egyptians."

In his statement after the Egyptian election results were announced, William Hague, the British secretary of foreign affairs, emphasized the need for an inclusive political process as well as greater accountability and transparency in Egyptian government. "We look to President-Elect Sisi to take steps to implement the rights contained in Egypt's constitution by opening up political space, especially in regard to freedom of expression and association," he stated. "We believe the best way for Egyptians to achieve the goals of the 25 January revolution of 2011 is through an inclusive political process in which all groups can participate. We urge Egypt's leaders to ensure that Egypt's transition leads towards accountable and democratic governance, underpinned by strong and accountable institutions."

National reconciliation and the inclusion of Islamic factions in the political system will continue to be pressing issues going forward in Egypt. The authors of the viewpoints in *Opposing Viewpoints: Egypt* ponder the recent political events in Egypt and examine the country's future in chapters titled "How Should Recent Political Events in Egypt Be Viewed?," "What Is the Impact of Recent Political and Social Upheaval in Egypt?," "What Political, Economic, and Social Policies Should Egypt Adopt?," and "What Should Be US Policy on Egypt?" The viewpoints in this volume provide information on the need for political, economic, and social reforms in Egypt; the critical problems that must be addressed by the new administration; and the direction the United States should consider in improving relations with Egypt in the future.

OPPOSING VIEWPOINTS® SERIES

CHAPTER 1

# How Should Recent Political Events in Egypt Be Viewed?

# Chapter Preface

On November 22, 2012, Egyptian president Mohamed Morsi outraged the Egyptian people by issuing a constitutional declaration that stripped the judiciary of its rights to challenge his decisions, thereby placing the president above judicial oversight. The directive declared that any laws, constitutional declarations, or decrees made by the president since he had taken office were "final and binding and cannot be appealed by any way or to any entity. Nor should they be suspended or canceled and all lawsuits related to them and brought before any judicial body against these decisions are annulled." Morsi was essentially giving himself near absolute power to rule the country.

The reaction was swift and strong. Tens of thousands of protesters took to the streets, deeming the declaration to be a power grab by Morsi and his political party, the Muslim Brotherhood, a conservative Islamist group. Senior Egyptian judges condemned the president's constitutional declaration, accusing him of launching an extraordinary attack on the nation's judiciary. They called for a nationwide strike, suspending work in all courts and judicial offices until the declaration was rescinded. Critics and political opponents accused Morsi of betraying the ideals of the Egyptian revolution, which had succeeded in overthrowing the dictatorship of President Hosni Mubarak in 2011 in favor of a more representative government that respected human rights and the rule of law.

Morsi's supporters defended the constitutional declaration, claiming it was needed to speed up the democratic transition and remove legal obstacles that had been hindering progress toward a democratic state. For many Egyptians, however, it raised concern that the hard-fought freedom they had earned from the 2011 protests and overthrow of the Mubarak regime was being ripped away from them.

As protests escalated in the following days and violent clashes between Morsi supporters and antigovernment protesters were broadcast on news programs around the world, Morsi's administration ignited more controversy. The Constituent Assembly, a panel dominated by Islamist allies of the president, pushed through a draft constitution that restricted freedom of speech, overlooked the issue of minority rights, and enhanced the role of Islamic law in civic life. It was also viewed as granting favor and political advantage to the Muslim Brotherhood. The panel formulated the draft constitution without the participation of liberal groups, Christian representatives, and women. A national vote on the controversial document was called for December 15, 2012.

Opposition to the Morsi administration spread and intensified after the announcement of the national referendum. Newspapers and privately owned television stations went on strike. Hundreds of thousands of protesters gathered in Tahrir Square. Several high-ranking politicians—and even some Morsi aides—resigned in protest over the declaration and the draft constitution.

Under mounting pressure, President Morsi rescinded most of the controversial constitutional declaration on December 10. He refused, however, to postpone the constitutional referendum to approve the constitution written by his Islamist supporters. Only 33 percent of the electorate voted in the referendum. The new constitution was approved with almost 64 percent.

After the vote, President Morsi appealed for an end to protests and called for national unity. He acknowledged that he had made mistakes during the process, but urged Egyptians to move forward together.

Egyptians were not willing to gamble that Morsi's administration would not consolidate its hold on government. By June 2013, it had become clear that the constitutional crisis that had sparked widespread protests was in danger of jeopardizing the country. Calls for Morsi's resignation got louder as protests grew. On July 1, the Egyptian military issued an ultimatum, giving the president forty-eight hours to settle his differences or be removed from office. Morsi refused. On July 3, Morsi was deposed, the new constitution was suspended, and an interim government was put in place until new democratic elections could be held.

The role of the military in Morsi's ouster is debated in the following chapter, which presents various perspectives on recent events in Egypt. Other viewpoints in the chapter examine the significance of the constitution approved in 2013 and address the controversy over whether the military takeover should be regarded as a military coup or a continuation of the Egyptian revolution that began in 2011.

> *"The coup restored the corrupt military/ bureaucratic class that has denied Egypt a modern government for half a century."*

# The Military Takeover of Egypt Should Be Deemed a Coup

*Robert Scheer*

*Robert Scheer is a journalist, political commentator, and editor of Truthdig. In the following viewpoint, he states that the Egyptian military's 2013 ouster of the democratically elected Egyptian president Mohamed Morsi should be regarded as a military coup undertaken with the approval of the United States government. Scheer considers the episode to be a gift to Islamists who did not believe that democratic elections were fair and would accurately reflect the will of the people. Instead, the military coup reinforces the belief of many in the Islamic world that lasting political change is better when it comes as a result of violent revolution instead of the ballot box. It is also a boon to Saudi Arabia, who did not want Egypt to have a functioning and vibrant democracy. Scheer predicts that Saudi Arabia and the United Arab Emirates will battle for influence over Egypt.*

As you read, consider the following questions:

1. According to Scheer, how much in aid does the United States provide to Egypt every year?

2. How does Scheer say that Egyptian interim prime minister Mohamed ElBaradei disgraced himself while talking about the military coup?

3. How many of the nineteen hijackers that participated in the September 11, 2001, terrorist attacks were from Saudi Arabia, according to the author?

The U.S. government has long been a hypocritical champion of democratic governance, claiming to honor free elections but historically attempting to subvert their outcomes when the result is not to our liking. But the rank betrayals of our commitment to the principles of representative democracy, from Guatemala to Iran to South Vietnam, among the scores of nations where we undermined duly elected leaders, reached a nadir with the coup by a U.S.-financed military in Egypt against that country's first democratically elected government.

## Facing the Truth

Embarrassingly, our law professor president [Barack Obama] refuses to label the arrest of Egypt's freely elected president by the military a coup because that would trigger an end to the $1.5 billion in U.S. aid as a matter of law. It remained for Sen. John McCain to set the president straight. "Reluctantly, I believe that we have to suspend aid until such time as there is a new constitution and a free and fair election," McCain said Sunday [July 7, 2013] on CBS's *Face the Nation*. Stating the obvious, he noted that, "It was a coup and it was the second time in two and a half years that we have seen the military step in. It is a strong indicator of a lack of American leadership and influence."

## July 3, 2013

On July 3, 2013, following several days of mass demonstrations against [Mohamed] Morsi's one-year rule, the Egyptian military unilaterally dissolved Morsi's government, suspended the constitution that had been passed during his rule, and installed the chief justice of the Supreme Constitutional Court, Judge Adly Mansour, as interim president pending a new election. In the days preceding the July 3 takeover, hundreds of thousands of Egyptians had flooded the streets of Cairo and elsewhere demanding Morsi's resignation, and clashes between the president's supporters and opponents had periodically turned deadly. The military, led by Defense Minister General Abdel Fattah al-Sisi, claimed that it had repeatedly encouraged Morsi to reconcile with his opponents to no avail. Sisi claimed that the military did not seek to rule the country directly. He empowered interim president and chief justice Mansour to issue constitutional declarations, establish a government of "technocrats," and form a commission to propose amendments to the constitution.

*Jeremy M. Sharp,*
*"Egypt: Background and U.S. Relations,"*
*Congressional Research Service, June 5, 2014.*

The Egyptian military would not have acted without at least the tacit approval of the U.S. government, and evidence is mounting that Secretary of State John Kerry and National Security Advisor Susan E. Rice were in on the plotting before President Mohamed Morsi was arrested. The bloodshed that has followed is on their hands, and lots of luck ever convincing Islamists anywhere of the value of free elections as opposed to violence as an enabler of change.

The coup restored the corrupt military/bureaucratic class that has denied Egypt a modern government for half a century. It was accompanied by the spectacle of Morsi's failed rivals in the last election rushing to offer their services as "democratic" replacements. They included the leaders of the Al-Nour Party, the one Islamic group that sided with the coup and that makes the Muslim Brotherhood seem quite moderate in comparison.

As for Nobel Peace Prize winner Mohamed ElBaradei and the others who claim to be human rights advocates, they stand condemned by their silence in the face of the president's arrest, the shutting down of an elected parliament, and the banning of media that might be the slightest bit critical of the military's seizure of power.

After the bloody Monday morning massacre of civilians at prayer by the heavily armed Egyptian military, interim prime minister ElBaradei disgraced himself by equating the violence of the armed with the resistance of the unarmed: "Violence begets violence and should be strongly condemned," he tweeted. "Independent investigation is a must." Not a word from this celebrated liberal concerning the military's stifling control over any avenue of investigation by the media or government.

The same charade of objectivity was on display in the response of U.S. State Department spokeswoman Jen Psaki, who, like ElBaradei, blithely equated the military's deadly excessive force with the rocks that soldiers claimed some of the demonstrators were throwing. "This is a situation where it's very volatile on the ground," she told reporters at a briefing Monday. "There are lots of parties contributing to that volatility."

## The Real Winners

The true victors of the coup are Mideast zealots who shun the ballot box as a rigged Western secular game, along with their sponsors in the bizarre theocracy of Saudi Arabia, the first country to welcome the downfall of Egypt's only serious attempt at representative governance. For all of the fanatical blather concerning Islam that has emanated from the oil-floated theocracy of Saudi Arabia, the spawning ground for Osama bin Laden and 15 of the 19 Sept. 11 [referring to the September 11, 2001, terrorist attacks on the United States] hijackers, it is the peaceful electoral campaigns of the populist-based Muslim Brotherhood that the Saudi royalty finds most threatening.

Now it is the turn of Saudi Arabia and the United Arab Emirates, both of which denied aid to Morsi's government, to reassert their influence over Egypt by rallying around the country's military. As the *Wall Street Journal* reported Monday, "Saudi Arabia and the U.A.E. are signaling they are prepared to start showering Egypt's new government with significant funding as it transitions away from Mr. Morsi and his Islamist movement."

So much for the promise of the Arab Spring; it will now be marketed as a franchise of the Saudi government. In the end, the argument was not secular versus religious, but rather whether power would reside in the ballot box or the barrel of the gun. The United States, and too many of Egypt's self-proclaimed secular democrats, ended up on the wrong side of that choice.

> "We should ask ourselves what rights we as Americans would accept losing before those stripping that which we consider inalienable are recognized as usurpers."

# The Military Takeover of Egypt Should Not Be Classified as a Coup

*Mark Ulrich*

*Mark Ulrich is a military officer and political analyst. In the following viewpoint, he argues that the 2013 ouster of democratically elected Mohamed Morsi in Egypt should be regarded as a successful effort to protect the country from the Muslim Brotherhood. Ulrich reports that once the Muslim Brotherhood was fairly elected and gained enough political power, it began to manipulate the democratic system in order to establish a sharia-based Islamic state—a process opposed by the majority of the Egyptian people. Morsi went as far as to assume full executive and legislative power, essentially making himself a dictator. Therefore, Ulrich maintains, the military takeover of the Egyptian government in 2013 was justified in order to protect the country from authoritarian rule. Ulrich contends that the United States should support Egypt by maintaining economic aid and encouraging a return to democratic principles.*

As you read, consider the following questions:

1. What three examples does the author give of insurgents merging into a legitimate political party?

2. Which Venezuelan president did Hugo Chávez unsuccessfully try to overthrow in 1992?

3. What American president does Ulrich cite as a figure taken for granted?

The big debate now, regarding Egypt, is whether the events of July 2013 should be classified as a coup d'état. The question becomes all the more divisive since U.S. foreign aid is rooted in the legality of a "no coup" policy. Much of the discussion, however, does not appear to be based on objective analysis, but is instead politically motivated with regard to foreign aid. Those opposing aid say it's a coup; those in favor say it's not. Common in the argument is justifying a coup via one-line dictionary definitions, like in Oxford "*a sudden, violent, and illegal seizure of power from a government.*" This, however, does not provide much analytical assessment of the purpose behind these events, which is necessary for this debate to have merit. What is missing is the larger narrative that describes coups in all their variations. For example, coups can be conducted by a small group of co-conspirators, or by a cadre backed by an entire insurgent movement. Even so, what happened in Egypt in July 2013 was not a coup but was in fact a counter-coup. The Muslim Brotherhood, an insurgent movement, conducted the actual coup d'état a year earlier when it manipulated the democratic process in order to establish a sharia-based Islamic state. The Egyptian military and much of the populace recognized and then reversed this coup. America, stable in its democracy, is poised to support Egypt as the troubled nation navigates its way through the tortuous political obstacles common in forming this type of government.

## Analyzing the Insurgency

Analysis of the insurgency's strategy and nature seems to be largely missing, at least in open debate, among pundits voicing opinions. The usual methods of analyzing insurgencies seem to focus merely on tactics and terrorism, completely dismissing the movement's nature and strategy. This absence of analytical rigor can lead to politically or economically driven courses of action or inaction, instead of a more prudent and lucid solution derived through understanding this form of irregular warfare. Mohamed Morsi, of the Muslim Brotherhood, was elected through a valid democratic process and therefore is the legitimate president of Egypt. This is true, but what many of those publicly debating this point may not realize is that the Muslim Brotherhood is an insurgent organization. Some may not accept this classification since, in more recent years, the Brotherhood has openly tried and succeeded in entering the political process and has denounced violence, even though they continue to export Islamist revolutions and subversive actions throughout the region. These actions are more predictable when assessment of an insurgency includes analysis of their strategy. The Muslim Brotherhood utilizes the 'subversive strategy' ... defined [as] *"either attempts to transform an illegal political entity into a legitimate political party or to use an existing legitimate political party. This party will attempt to subvert the government from within."* The nature of this insurgency, through the use of the subversive strategy, is to transform the secular Egyptian government to that of an Islamic theocracy. A major difference between a subversive strategy and a violent coup or abrupt overthrow is that these changes are subtle and gradual, appearing to follow the accepted and legitimate political process.

The subversive strategy is used when a group is unsuccessful in sneaking or breaking in the back door of a government and instead tricks their way through the front door. This strategy centers on the insurgent's political wing becoming a legitimate party which can enter the political process. Examples include Sinn Féin of the IRA [Irish Republican Army], Hezbollah in Lebanon, and most recently the Taliban in Qatar. This party can then carry out seemingly normal political activities, while deriving support from illegal or illegitimate actions by other wings of the insurgency. These activities, designed to appear normal and favorable, may include reintegration of insurgent members back into society, which are instead deliberate and calculated steps towards eventual destruction of the government from within. Some urged and continue to argue that the Muslim Brotherhood be included in the process as opposed to being opponents. Inclusion is only useful if repatriation or collaboration of the organization's members is the true intent. In the analysis of a movement, using specific methodologies such as the dynamics of insurgency, referenced in U.S. Army Field Manual 3-24 *counterinsurgency*, helps decipher the type of insurgency, its strategy, and the condition of the movement. The point is that insurgents do not commit to reconciliation from a functioning subversive strategy and from a position of strength like the Muslim Brotherhood was at the time of the anti-Mubarak [referring to former Egyptian president Hosni Mubarak] riots and follow-on elections. Instead reintegration-type actions are done when an insurgent movement is weak and fracturing. No one says, "We're winning! . . . Let's quit."

## An Insidious Process

If an insurgency successfully enters the government, and continues to follow the subversive model, many follow-on events are generally predictable. Looking at the insurgent's ideology, goals, and capabilities provides a means to deduce how they plan on accomplishing their goals. An insurgent who wanted to change Egypt into an Islamic state under sharia law would need to change the constitution, suspend rights, and manipulate the judicial, military, and political systems. Judges and legislators who do not cooperate would have to be intimidated or fired. The use of referendums to help justify changing the constitution may be used if many people are generally dissatisfied and plied with things like heavy propaganda, bribes, and intimidation. Opponents and the media need to be silenced and more insurgents or supporters need to be brought into the government. If an insurgent actually becomes head of state, even if done completely within the bounds of the law, the strategy moves into its final stages by deliberately dismantling that form of government from the top.

Hugo Chávez, the recently deceased presidential dictator of Venezuela, draws an interesting parallel to the current issues in Egypt. President Chávez, a military officer and founder of the secretive socialist Movimiento Bolivariano Revolucionario 200 (MBR-200), had a goal to overthrow, through coup, the Carlos Andrés Pérez presidency in 1992. Although these attempts failed and Chávez was arrested, he became famous, was later pardoned, and then successfully ran for public office through legitimate means. As president, he changed the constitution, suspended free press, and other actions common to this strategy to affect the same types of changes that he would have enacted if he had been victorious in the original overthrow.

## Morsi's Rise and Fall

In the case of Egypt, Morsi began ordering the release of hundreds of prisoners and pardoned dozens of convicted hardliner Islamists from the Muslim Brotherhood and Al-Gama'a al-Islamiyya, which is considered to be a terrorist organization by the United States and the European Union. Morsi began removing his opponents from their posts like Egypt's intelli-

# The Origins of the Muslim Brotherhood

Many contemporary terrorist groups of the Middle East have roots in the Muslim Brotherhood.... The Muslim Brotherhood was not initially a terrorist organization, but by the 1940s some of its members began using acts of violence as a method of promoting their political cause. The movement spread rapidly throughout the Middle East, starting in the 1950s. At that time, another conflict was brewing that would eventually lead to terrorist activities. Jews established the State of Israel in Palestine ... and the 1948 Arab-Israeli War erupted in response. During that war, hundreds of thousands of the Arab Palestinians, people who had lived for centuries on the land that Israel claimed, were forced to flee their homes and livelihoods. Many of the Palestinian refugees relocated to refugee camps in the West Bank, an area on the west bank of the Jordan River that was part of Jordan; in the Gaza Strip, a narrow strip of land along the eastern shore of the Mediterranean Sea that was part of Egypt; and in other neighboring Arab countries. Palestinians continued to press their claim to territory within the former region of Palestine, but for a time, they were too poor and poorly organized to fight the powerful Israeli army. By the 1970s, however, Palestinians had begun to organize. Some Palestinians joined local Muslim Brotherhood branches, and in places like the Gaza Strip and Lebanon, the objectives of the two groups were combined.

*Jennifer Stock, ed.*
*"Terrorism Based in the Middle East," Middle East Conflict*
*Reference Library. Farmington Hills, MI: UXL, 2012.*

gence chief, several ministers, and a governor and replacing them with allies from his organization and the aforementioned Al-Gama'a al-Islamiyya. It may appear to be normal for political leaders to bring in members of their own party to the government, however, the Brotherhood is an insurgency and the goal is not to form an effective transitional democratic government, but instead to destroy it in favor of an exclusive sharia law–based regime. Morsi continued extralegal moves, in the spirit and doctrine of the subversive strategy, by replacing the military's top leadership, attempting to remove a leading prosecutor, proclaiming he was taking full executive and legislative power, and stating he was now beyond the reach of Egypt's judicial checks and balances.

Eventually, Morsi made several overt missteps by moving too fast in his dismantling of Egypt's system of government. By doing so, he and the Muslim Brotherhood became exposed as conspirators against democracy. This started with many opposition representatives resigning in protest and announcing that Morsi's Islamists, in large numbers, had subverted the constitutional drafting committee and were openly turning the nation away from being a republic. Additionally, Morsi's hasty actions to intimidate the press backfired and he was forced to openly renounce his own administration's arbitrary arrests of reporters declaring his support for public opposition, something generally incongruous with extremist Islamic regimes. He pushed to limit the freedom to demonstrate and thwart free expression by way of "secret police," a subversive tactic reminiscent of the strategy's namesake. An example of this occurred during demonstrations in December 2012, when witnesses recount the arrests, detention, and beatings of protesters by members of the Muslim Brotherhood. This paramilitary element, in insurgent speak, is referred to as the movement's 'underground' and the activity is referred to as 'populace and resource control operations.' Underground members are not commonly used this overtly as most of their activities are covert or clandestine by nature. Since changing the constitution is generally critical in the subversive strategy, it is not unpredictable for a movement to assume risk and use their underground to openly block opposition.

In the cases of Hugo Chávez and Mohamed Morsi, these insurgent leaders manipulated their way into the legitimate political process to gain entry, utilizing the subversive insurgent strategy, in order to change the constitutions, consolidate extraordinary powers, and remove opposition members all in an effort to overthrow the legitimate democratic system of government. What the Egyptian Armed Forces did was counter the Muslim Brotherhood's coup d'état. Mohamed Morsi violated his oath while the military followed theirs: "*I swear to be a loyal Soldier to the Arab Republic of Egypt, preserving and defending it, on land, sea and air, preserving the republic system. I will never leave my gun till death. I swear and my God is a witness.*" Coups d'état are not the job of the military; "preserving the republic system" is their job, and they followed their oath.

## Setting Egypt on Its Rightful Path

As we debate whether or not Egypt's military conducted a coup against a legitimate democratic president in the summer of 2013, we should ask ourselves what rights we as Americans would accept losing before those stripping that which we consider inalienable are recognized as usurpers and would impel the people and the military to return the government to its foundation. We just celebrated our 237th year of independence, and enjoy a very stable government with a steadfast system of checks and balances, but have we forgotten our own uncertain beginnings? At times, we take for granted the fact that without George Washington removing a king, refusing to be a king, and later guiding our new nation as the president, we might not have succeeded in this 'great experiment.' The problem is men like George Washington are, like his predecessor and sole peer Cincinnatus [a Roman statesman known for putting the greater good before his personal ambition], rare.

There may be some still willing to hang their entire argument on the fact that Morsi was duly elected and therefore there is no legal remedy until the next election. Does this mean that the election is the only characteristic of a democracy, regardless of Morsi's conduct to oppress political opposition, manipulate the constitution, and violate individual rights? The Egyptian military, backed by the people, preserved their nation, countered the Muslim Brotherhood's insurgent coup, and reclaimed their country. By doing so, the Egyptian people have made a clear statement that they reject authoritarian rule and favor a democracy, at least for now. Opportunities to assist nascent democracies are infrequent enough, especially in that region. These events should signal the United States to embrace and support the struggling democratic nation, as opposed to allowing the insurgents to regroup and reorganize amid the confusion and unrest, while we debate our short-term agendas in the name of political righteousness.

> "Debates are already raging over whether the events . . . can be fairly described as a coup or not, as the subversion of democracy or its expression."

# Is What Happened in Egypt a Coup or a Revolution? It's Both

*Max Fisher*

*Max Fisher is a journalist. In the following viewpoint, he maintains that the July 2013 military takeover of Egypt meets the definition of both a coup and a continuation of the 2011 revolution. Fisher argues that the events of July 2013 could be described as "both a coup and a popular movement, both the expression and subversion of Egypt's democratic experiment." He worries that because the events were so divisive and viewed so differently by those on the opposite sides of the political spectrum in Egypt that there is little room for citizens to come together to move the country forward. He deems it essential that both sides of the standoff acknowledge how the country got to that point*

*and the implications of the political and social upheaval that re-
sulted. If that doesn't happen, Fisher predicts that the unrest in
Egypt could very well continue in the future.*

As you read, consider the following questions:

1. How long was Egyptian president Mohamed Morsi in
   power, according to Fisher?

2. When does the author say that Egypt's struggle began?

3. According to Fisher, what Egyptian dictator was ousted
   in 2011?

When Egyptian military chief Abdel Fattah al-Sisi went
on Egyptian TV Wednesday [in July 2013] to read the
statement that ended President Mohamed Morsi's one-year
tenure, observers within and [outside of] Egypt seemed to
hear one of two very different events.

Some, often those who opposed Morsi and saw his rule as
increasingly undemocratic, cheered at the announcement that
he would be replaced by the head of the constitutional court
until early elections could be held. They saw the will of the
people, expressed through mass protests numbering perhaps
in the millions, finally fulfilled. But others saw a nation's fate
decided by a khaki-clad general, a military coup under the veneer of popular support. And, for them, a few words in Sisi's
statement jumped out in a way that it may not have for others: "the constitution is suspended."

Debates are already raging over whether the events of July
3 can be fairly described as a coup or not, as the subversion of
democracy or its expression. Those debates are largely academic; what happened could be said to meet the definition of
a coup, as well as that of a revolution. But even though both
words might apply, neither is in itself enough to describe what
happened: It was both a coup and a popular movement, both
the expression and subversion of Egypt's democratic experi-

ment. And, as *Foreign Policy*'s Joshua Keating points out, although some academic literature finds that coups can be democratizing that doesn't make them democratic.

But it's not easy, especially for those Egyptians who have invested and lost so much in their country's struggle since January 2011, to see both sides. Many, particularly Morsi's supporters within the still-vast Muslim Brotherhood, will likely see July 3 as little more than a military coup, the return of decades of military rule that always loathed the Brotherhood. Activists who opposed Morsi will surely continue to insist that the military stepped in only to safeguard the people's will from Morsi himself.

Few Egyptian activists invested in Wednesday's events on either side of the political spectrum will likely want to acknowledge the breadth of what happened—as few have been willing to acknowledge both that Morsi possessed the mandate of a popular democratic election and that he had eroded much of that mandate by his own actions. Yes, the United States continued to deal with him and to describe him as the democratically elected leader; yes, he at times undermined democratic institutions and often excluded non-Islamists, neither of which did much to live up to the mandate Morsi often used to justify his behavior.

It's a cliché within U.S. politics to point out that the two ends of the political divide see different versions of the same reality and will never be able to accomplish anything until they can find a middle ground. But, in Egypt, this is deadly true, with one important distinction: The two "sides" to this political dispute are seeing the same reality—they're both right—but each is only able or willing to look at half.

That leaves the other half to imagination, and both Morsi's supporters and detractors had turned increasingly to conspiracy theories to explain the situation. Many in Egypt's opposition, unwilling to acknowledge any scrap of legitimacy for the Morsi government or the possibility that he enjoyed some real base of support, blamed his perseverance on clandestine American support. And Morsi's government, ironically enough, accused U.S.-funded NGOs [nongovernmental organizations] of fomenting the Egyptian opposition movements, which Morsi seemed unwilling to believe could be rooted in legitimate gripes.

So, were the events of July 3 a coup, or were they a second iteration of the February 2011 revolution? Was democracy expressed, or was it subverted? The answer is "both." If Egypt is going to deal with this transition much better than 2011, it might well require both sides of this week's standoff to acknowledge the full extent of July 3 and how the country got to that point. The Muslim Brotherhood, which is influential enough that it will likely remain a real political force, has some significant lessons to learn about political inclusion and legitimacy; it would not be easy for the group to ask itself if it really did squander its presidency, but they've endured much harder times than this.

A lesson for opponents of the Brotherhood, though, may be that the Islamist group didn't get to the presidency by accident and will not disappear. The Muslim Brotherhood has proven one of Egypt's most organized and effective political organizations. For the military and others to treat a coup that deposed the Brotherhood's president as a non-coup and democratic event leaves the Brotherhood little real space in Egyptian politics. That would seem to risk a repeat of the same problem that plagued and ultimately ousted Morsi—except instead of an Islamist ruler acting as if non-Islamists had no right to participate, it would be the other way around.

Similarly, to insist that what happened in Egypt was not a coup would leave the door open for the military to depose any ruler it feels has lost sufficient political legitimacy; even if you think the generals got it right this time around, will you still agree next time?

Flash back to February 2011, when cheering crowds received the news that President Hosni Mubarak was leaving office. It wasn't until several months later that observers started to wonder if it had really been a revolution that had toppled Mubarak, or a military coup. His resignation, after all, had been announced by one of the top generals who soon took interim rule. Tanks had been in the streets. Were events primarily driven by popular will, as expressed by thousands or millions of protesters, or by the powerful military?

That distinction is not much more obvious today than it was then. And, unless something changes in the Egyptian political culture that allows one part of the country to see two dramatically different versions of the same event, it's a distinction they may end up revisiting.

> *"The overthrow of the Muslim Brotherhood is an exercise of the will of the Egyptian people, and it was a necessary action to advance the country's hopes for prosperity and democracy."*

# Egypt's Military Coup Was a Legitimate Expression of the People's Will

*Reese Neader*

*Reese Neader is a political activist and commentator; he is also the founder and director of Forge Columbus, a civic innovation program. In the following viewpoint, he recalls his experience in Egypt in 2011 and provides his perspective on the 2013 military takeover. Neader asserts that the overthrow of the Muslim Brotherhood was not a coup because it represented the will of the majority of Egyptian people. Therefore, it should be seen as a legitimate expression of democracy. In Neader's view, the military's role has been to protect democracy and the gains made through the 2011 revolution. With the ouster of President Mohamed Morsi and the Muslim Brotherhood, the military exercised the*

*will of the Egyptian people. He concludes that it is vital that the
United States continue to provide much-needed economic aid to
Egypt.*

As you read, consider the following questions:

1. According to the viewpoint, why was Neader sent to
   Egypt by the US State Department?

2. According to the author, how much does the US government invest in the Egyptian military every year?

3. How much has a coalition of Gulf States pledged to assist the new Egyptian government, according to Neader?

In the summer of 2011 I was serving as policy director for
the Roosevelt Institute Campus Network, organizing thousands of students across the U.S. to build community change.
2011 was also the year of the Egyptian revolution. Inspired
youth had banded together across the country and across ideologies to protest and overthrow the dictatorship of Hosni
Mubarak. Because I had a proven background in youth organizing, the State Department sent me to Egypt in late July
2011 under their "Speakers and Specialists" program to train
youth opposition leaders in grassroots organizing and political
communication and to support Egypt's hopeful transition to
democracy. What I learned there has made me more optimistic about the ousting of President Mohamed Morsi than many
other Americans.

## A Perspective on Egypt

It was a deeply humbling and life-changing experience, and
thankfully I've managed to keep in touch with some of the
friends I made during my travels. To honor their friendship
and support a sensible response to the recent coup in Egypt, I
want to speak out against the false narrative that Egypt is experiencing the "death of democracy." In truth, Egypt's military

has served as the guardian of the Egyptian revolution. The overthrow of the Muslim Brotherhood is an exercise of the will of the Egyptian people, and it was a necessary action to advance the country's hopes for prosperity and democracy.

The most important thing to remember as you watch events unfold in Egypt is that the United States government invests more than $1 billion a year in the Egyptian military. The Egyptian military has a very deep relationship with the U.S. military and a massive ownership stake in Egypt's economy. It will never act strongly against the interests of the United States because it cannot afford to lose its support. For the same reasons, the Egyptian military, as well as the civilian elite of the country, want Egypt to be a stable, prosperous, and moderate Islamic republic that is closely aligned with the United States.

Clearly that insight doesn't speak to the concerns of Americans who view the recent coup in Egypt as the disruption of burgeoning democracy. But those concerns misconstrue the reality of what happened in Egypt in 2011. The Egyptian revolution was a popular coup overseen by the Egyptian military. Egypt's military leadership guided the transition to civilian governance by forging a power-sharing agreement with the Muslim Brotherhood after they won elections that were overseen by a provisional government controlled by the Egyptian military. Yes, it is true that the Brotherhood and other hard-line Islamist groups won a landslide popular vote in mostly free and fair elections. But their victory wasn't the result of popular democratic mobilization as we think about it here in the U.S. The Muslim Brotherhood is an extremist group that has a tremendous advantage at organizing political support in a country rife with economic and social poverty.

## The Appeal of Extremism

In the developing world, extremism thrives in places where people have nothing to lose and nowhere to go. Where gov-

# The Decline of Islamist Extremism?

In the last quarter of the twentieth century, Islamic extremism had grown into one of the most potent forces in the Middle East. During that era, there were few political movements for the general public in the Middle East to join. The governments of the Middle East were mainly authoritarian, meaning that power was consolidated under one strong leader, or a small group of elite leaders, and the people who lived there had little voice in their governments and could not freely oppose them. Militant groups like al-Qaeda arose during a time of frustration with the Western powers and Israel, and the frustration was also a product of the lack of political freedom in most Middle Eastern countries. By 2011, though, many analysts questioned whether al-Qaeda's network was still as much of a threat as it had been in the past. When the Middle East became swept up in the Arab Spring in 2011, the people of the Middle East called for democracy. Modernization, particularly the rise of communication through the Internet, allowed political expression in a way that was impossible only a decade earlier. There seemed to be little public interest in trying to recapture the glories of the seventh-century Islamic empire. Although few believed that terrorist groups like al-Qaeda would stop terrorizing, many political experts expressed a cautious hope that there would be fewer fires to ignite militant movements with the opening up of political expression in the Middle East.

*Jennifer Stock, ed.*
*"Terrorism Based in the Middle East," Middle East Conflict*
*Reference Library. Farmington Hills, MI: UXL, 2012.*

ernments fail to serve their citizens, informal support networks arise to provide the basic services that the government does not: food, jobs, education, health care. And in exchange for providing those services, extremist organizations demand total loyalty from the citizens they service. Hamas and Hezbollah are both terrorist organizations that have been democratically elected to represent the territories they control, not because the citizens of Gaza and Lebanon are supportive of Islamic extremism, but because they depend on these patronage networks.

Similarly, the Muslim Brotherhood has been organizing in the neighborhoods of Egypt for over 50 years, providing social services that the government did not in an effort to win support for its ideology. And it, along with other Islamist groups like the Salafis, was the only organized opposition to the Mubarak dictatorship. When Mubarak was deposed, and there was a popular call for swift elections, who was going to win? It was never a question: the only organized opposition group that had a proven track record of providing services to the people.

The Muslim Brotherhood's extreme incompetence at governing was dividing the country along sectarian lines and led Egypt to the brink of a severe economic crisis. While the citizens of Egypt grew desperate from economic hardship and social strain, the Egyptian military elite grew concerned with the direction of civilian governance and orchestrated a takeover that will minimize casualties and guide the country toward economic growth and stable, moderate democratic governance.

## We Must Aid Egypt

Currently, there is bipartisan clamoring for the suspension of foreign aid to Egypt. While it is highly likely that these are hollow threats, the suspension of foreign aid to Egypt would be disastrous for U.S. geopolitical interests in the region. U.S.

aid to Egypt ensures a strong military partnership, tacit influence over the direction of Egyptian governance, and peace and high-level cooperation between Egypt and Israel. Giving up that leverage because a popular revolt deposed a radical Islamist government would be a tremendous blow to our long-term interests in the region.

The U.S. government pays lip service to supporting democratic mobilization in the Middle East. If it wants to do this without creating instability that extremists can use to their advantage, we need to build relationships with regional leaders to forge civil society and support strong economic growth. And that will inherently involve "choosing sides." Anyone in the West who thinks that the Arab world is defined by popular support for radical Islamism needs only look to the massive protests that destroyed the Muslim Brotherhood. The people of the Middle East want economic opportunity, democratic representation, and integration with the global community.

In response to the coup, the Gulf States (staunch U.S. allies) have pledged $12 billion in assistance to the new Egyptian government. This will allow the provisional government, which is being directed by Western-educated, liberal technocrats, to continue the provision of desperately needed public subsidies while providing an infusion of cash for investment in job creation. Already, the Egyptian military is in the process of organizing another constitutional convention and continuing to support the construction of a provisional government that will lead the country toward adoption of the national blueprint for governance drafted by civilian authorities.

Instead of decrying the "death of democracy" and publicly scolding Egypt's military leadership, the United States needs to react with patience and calm support. It is easy for us to forget that democracy is never easy and the process is always messy. The massive wave of protests that brought down the Muslim Brotherhood represents the will of the Egyptian people. In the eyes of the people of Egypt, their revolution continues. We should respect their voice. *Vox Populi, Vox Dei—* the voice of the people is the voice of God.

> "*I guess that Western leaders are making the cynical but—as they see it— realistic judgment that a military regime . . . is the best hope of stability.*"

# Egypt's Military Coup Is Illegitimate and Undemocratic

*Peter Osborne*

*Peter Osborne is a journalist, author, political commentator, and associate editor of the* Spectator, *a conservative magazine. In the following viewpoint, he describes a recent troubling trip to Egypt, during which he observed growing lawlessness and social upheaval as well as stifling political repression. Osborne views the leader of Egypt's military junta, General Abdel Fattah al-Sisi, as a potential dictator and maintains that the 2013 military takeover of the Egyptian government was illegitimate. In his opinion, ousted president Mohamed Morsi was democratically elected and the military had no right to depose him. He derides Western governments as complicit in the military's blatantly undemocratic actions in Egypt. He also points out that the growing political oppression in Egypt will only lead to resurgence of Islamic terrorist activity and may convince the supporters of the Muslim Brotherhood to turn to violence instead of political legitimacy.*

As you read, consider the following questions:

1. According to Osborne, what part of the national penal code did the military junta use to ban the Muslim Brotherhood as a terrorist organization?

2. How many Egyptian protesters have been shot in the street by military and police forces since the 2013 coup, according to the viewpoint?

3. In what three elections was the Muslim Brotherhood democratically elected in Egypt, according to the author?

The earliest political decision made by Ayman al-Zawahiri, the Egyptian doctor who has presided over such a dramatic resurgence of al-Qaeda since Osama bin Laden's death, was to join the Muslim Brotherhood.

Even then, back in the mid-sixties, the Brotherhood was proscribed. This meant that it was impossible for a young man like Zawahiri to get involved in mainstream politics. Instead, Egypt's brutally repressive system of government forced him down the path that led to al-Qaeda and the Twin Towers [referring to the September 11, 2001, terrorist attacks on the United States].

## The Situation in Egypt

Is history about to repeat itself? I ask this urgent question because I have just returned from a very troubling trip to Cairo, a city that I last visited in the summer of 2011. Everything seemed possible back then, when the crowds gathered in Tahrir Square during the hopeful, happy, good-natured months that followed the fall of President [Hosni] Mubarak.

Today, protest is punishable by jail. Abductions are commonplace, torture routine. Demonstrators get shot dead. Following the coup that removed President [Mohamed] Morsi on July 3 last year [2013], a military junta is in control. Acting president Adly Mansour is a puppet. The defence minister, General [Abdel Fattah al-]Sisi, runs the country.

© Malcolm McGookin/Cartoonstock.com.

Looking much younger than his 59 years, he has become a sex symbol for middle-aged Egyptian ladies. His picture is everywhere—in shops, in cafes, on street corners. Very often General Sisi appears in posters alongside [Gamal Abdel] Nasser and [Anwar] Sadat, two previous military strongmen. He is expected to stand for president in elections to be held on an unspecified date this year. He has reportedly told friends of a series of visions, some dating back decades, in which it was divulged to him that he is destined to emerge as Egypt's saviour.

## The Campaign Against the Muslim Brotherhood

Meanwhile, what of the Brotherhood, which won the presidency in free and fair elections only 18 months ago? On Christmas Day, the military junta used article 86 of the national penal code to ban it as a terrorist organisation. The excuse was a bomb attack carried out by the Sinai-based terrorist group Ansar Bayt al-Maqdis ("Supporters of Jerusalem") on a police station in the northern town of Mansoura, which claimed 16 lives.

Ansar Bayt are long-standing opponents of the Brotherhood, having once attacked Morsi as an "unbeliever". Never mind: anyone who attends one of the Brotherhood's protest marches now faces five years in prison. Its supporters can no longer appear on TV, indeed, only those who concur with the official view that the Muslim Brotherhood is a terrorist organisation are allowed on air.

The entire leadership is now either in jail, or hiding, or fled the country. The organisation has retreated to the secret cell structure used to protect itself during previous periods of repression. Meetings now take place in private homes: The only objective is survival, and there are suggestions that even the cell structure has been compromised.

I did not try to meet anyone from the Brotherhood during my visit, and not just because of fears for my own safety— though I could easily have ended up in jail alongside three journalists from Al Jazeera who were picked up late last month. I was rather more worried about the consequences for anyone I approached.

President Morsi (I prefer to call him by that name, since the military coup that displaced him was not just illegal but immoral) is in prison. He was meant to face trumped-up charges in court in Cairo yesterday, but did not appear. The authorities mysteriously blamed "bad weather": it was fine both in Alexandria, where Morsi is in jail, and in Cairo.

## The Western Reaction

Britain, Europe and the United States, while not directly involved, have been complicit in much of this. Presumably afraid, as so often, to annoy the Americans, [British secretary of foreign affairs] William Hague has yet even to utter the phrase "coup d'état". Indeed, he immediately recognised the new regime. [US secretary of state] John Kerry went even further. In an interview on Pakistani TV in August, he hailed General Sisi for "restoring democracy" and praised him for averting violence.

These remarks from the secretary of state went beyond satire. Well over 1,000 protesters have been shot dead in the streets, the bloodiest encounter coming at the Rabaa al-Adawiya mosque in Cairo last August, when more than 600 people were killed.

Egyptian police are well practised in crowd control and the use of rubber bullets. It can therefore be assumed that the mass killing was deliberate. According to survivors, more than 20 people were run over by a police bulldozer. So far, General Sisi's regime has made no attempt to investigate these crimes. During my brief stay, I met a few of the journalists who have attempted to go out and tell the truth: They are very brave.

Since my return, I have been trying to make sense of British and American policy. I guess that Western leaders are making the cynical but—as they see it—realistic judgment that a military regime led by Sisi is the best hope of stability. In the short term, that might be right. But in the longer term, I wonder.

## Beware of the Consequences

Let's revisit the story of Ayman al-Zawahiri, driven underground by the Nasserite reign of terror 50 years ago. For several years, one of the biggest selling points for al-Qaeda, the organisation he now runs, was the claim that the Western powers would never allow democracy in the Muslim world—meaning that there was no alternative to armed struggle. The men of violence pointed to the democratic victory of Islamist parties in Algeria in 1992, who were brought down at once by a military coup, followed by a decade of civil war.

The Muslim Brotherhood rejected this analysis, and spent eight decades plodding towards power. Eventually, it secured it peacefully, having come out on top in three separate tests of popular opinion—the parliamentary elections of January 2012, the presidential elections of May and June 2012, and the constitutional referendum that December. It has now been declared a terrorist organisation.

The Brotherhood's leaders continue to preach nonviolence. But will all their followers agree to wait another 80 years before winning power through democratic means? A number are bound to turn to violence. Already, parts of the Sinai are starting to resemble northern Syria, Benghazi in Libya or Anbar province in Iraq—ungovernable havens for militant groups.

## Great Britain Must Lead

Britain cannot take sides in the great civil conflict that engulfs Egypt. But we can surely sustain the values that we claim to cherish. Thus far, our response has been poor, and will remain a blot on William Hague's record as foreign secretary.

This week, a group of lawyers claiming to represent President Morsi and the Muslim Brotherhood asked the International Criminal Court to investigate crimes against humanity committed by all sides during the course of the revolution. Since the Sisi regime shows no appetite to investigate the killings, Britain should support this request. Since the Brotherhood continues to demonstrate its faith in Western concepts of justice and democracy, it would be more than polite to return the compliment. It would also be sensible and wise. There's an old Egyptian doctor, hiding out somewhere on the Pakistan-Afghan border, who would be more than happy to let General Sisi just get on with it.

> "[Egyptians] voted for the new constitution in order to express their opposition to the Muslim Brotherhood and their support for the military."

# Egypt's New Constitution Is a Step Toward Democracy

*Hafez Ghanem*

*Hafez Ghanem is a senior fellow in the Global Economy and Development program at the Brookings Institution. In the following viewpoint, he regards the approval of the new Egyptian Constitution in January 2014 as a major step toward a democratic future for the nation. Ghanem contends that the 2014 constitution holds several improvements over the one passed in 2012, including limiting the role of Islam in politics, allowing for more freedom of speech, and ensuring more rights and protections for women. He believes that the popularity of the military leadership and the overwhelming response to the constitutional referendum show the country's rejection of the Muslim Brotherhood and its support for Egypt's democratic future. The process of democratization in Egypt may take some time because of the country's weak democratic institutions and its limited experience with democracy. The new constitution is a key first step, Ghanem concludes.*

As you read, consider the following questions:

1. According to Ghanem, what was the participation rate in the January 2014 constitutional referendum in Egypt?

2. When does the author say that the Muslim Brotherhood was declared a terrorist organization?

3. What year was the Muslim Brotherhood founded, according to Ghanem?

The approval of a new constitution in a referendum that took place on January 14–15, 2014, is an important step in implementing the road map announced by the current interim authorities in Egypt. The authorities feel that it provides them with greater legitimacy. After all, the participation rate of nearly 39 percent and the 98 percent yes vote are higher than those obtained by the Muslim Brotherhood–backed 2012 constitution, which had a participation rate of 33 percent and a yes vote of 64 percent.

According to the preliminary assessment of Transparency International, ". . . the political context in the run-up to the referendum impaired conditions to hold a fair and free referendum when compared with international standards." The assessment pointed out that the interim authorities took some steps that limited freedom of expression, association and assembly, and that the space for civil society to represent the voice of the people has been greatly reduced. The Muslim Brotherhood was declared a terrorist organisation in December 2013. According to Transparency International, government officials as well as public and private media outlets campaigned vigorously for a 'yes' vote and did not provide an opportunity for the opposition to express their views. Moreover, activists who called for a 'no' vote or for boycotting the referendum faced repression.

In spite of these problems, nearly all foreign observers seem to agree that what is going on in Egypt now is very popular among Egyptians. Why do a majority of Egyptians support the new constitution and the repression of the Brotherhood? What does this imply for Egypt's future?

## The New Constitution

The new constitution presents some improvements over the Brotherhood's constitution of 2012. First, it curtails the role of Islam in legislation and politics. Sharia is reaffirmed as the principal source of legislation, but a controversial article that gave religious leaders the right to interpret is removed. It also bans political parties based on religion. Second, it provides for equality of sexes. In the Brotherhood's constitution, the article referring to traditional Egyptian family was removed.

Instead, language was added to ensure equal rights in all civil, political, economic, social and cultural matters, including women's right to participate in government and be protected from gender-based violence. Third, it includes stronger language on human rights. It provides more latitude for freedom of speech and bans discrimination based on religion or beliefs. It also outlaws torture and arbitrary forced displacement.

The new constitution as well as the Brotherhood's 2012 constitution are criticised by pro-democracy activists for the special status they provide to the military establishment. Both constitutions limit parliamentary oversight of the military budget, which will appear in the national budget as one line item. Moreover, both constitutions allow for the trial of civilians by military courts under certain conditions. The new constitution also added a provisional article that states that for the next eight years, the Supreme Council of the Armed Forces (which consists of the most senior officers) will have to approve the selection of the minister of defence.

## Reinforcing Egyptian Nationalism

Discussions with ordinary Egyptians who supported the new constitution seem to indicate that the content of the constitu-

---

### 2014 Constitutional Vote in Figures

| | |
|---|---|
| Total registered voters: | 53,423,485 |
| Turnout: | 20,613,677 (38.6 percent) |
| Invalid votes: | 246,947 |
| Yes: | 19,985,389 (98.1 percent) |
| No: | 381,341 (1.9 percent) |

TAKEN FROM: "Official Vote Result: 98.1% Approves Egypt's Post-June 30 Constitution," Ahram Online, January 18, 2014.

---

tion was not the main issue. They voted for the new constitution in order to express their opposition to the Muslim Brotherhood and their support for the military, particularly for its charismatic leader, General Abdel Fattah al-Sisi. Ordinary Egyptians who normally are not interested in politics distrust the Brotherhood, as they worry that political Islam is inconsistent with Egyptian nationalism. The Brotherhood's performance during the year they were in power has apparently confirmed their fears.

Egyptians are very nationalistic, as they see themselves as the representatives of one of the world's most ancient civilisations and nation-states. Modern nationalist sentiment in Egypt dates back to the late 19th century when Ahmed Orabi, at the time head of the Egyptian armed forces, revolted in 1879 against the Khedive, who represented the Ottoman Empire. Orabi's 'revolution' failed as the British intervened to support the Khedive. Nevertheless, Orabi continues to be a revered figure in Egypt as the first nationalist leader in modern history. He established two traditions: Egyptian nationalism in conflict with pan-Islamism, which was represented by the Ottoman Empire at that time, and the Egyptian military as a bastion of nationalist sentiment. [Gamal Abdel] Nasser and [Anwar] Sadat, two nationalist presidents of the post-colonial period, had a military background and could be seen as the successors of Orabi. General al-Sisi comes from the same tradition, and many anti-Brotherhood demonstrations today raise pictures of Nasser next to those of al-Sisi.

The Muslim Brotherhood could be considered as the antithesis of Egyptian nationalism. It was created in 1928 as a pan-Islamic social and political movement, partly in response to the fall of the Ottoman Empire and the abolition of the Caliphate by [Mustafa Kemal] Atatürk, which was seen as an important setback by pious Muslims who considered the Caliphate as a necessity in Islam. The Brotherhood views Egypt as just one small part of a large Islamic Caliphate stretching from Spain to Indonesia. A previous general guide of the Brotherhood (Mohammed Akef) generated an outcry when he said in one of his interviews "to hell with Egypt." He only meant to emphasise the pan-Islamic ambitions of his organisation, but his statement was interpreted by nationalists as "the Brotherhood does not care for Egypt".

## Morsi's Misrule

The Brotherhood failed to assuage nationalists' fears during its one year in power. Egyptians were suspicious of the special relations that the Brotherhood built with Turkey, Qatar and Hamas. The Brotherhood was not forceful in denying rumours (not supported by any evidence) that it was selling rights to the Suez Canal to Qatar and was giving special privileges to Hamas in the Sinai. Concomitantly, the Brotherhood attacked important bastions of nationalism such as the judiciary and the cultural/artistic elites. The judges club was in an open conflict with the Brotherhood and claimed that they were undermining the independence of the judiciary. And, Egypt's influential artists, writers and filmmakers started an open-ended sit-in in front of the Ministry of Culture to protest Islamists' restrictions on freedom of artistic expression and creativity.

Many Egyptians did not believe in the Brotherhood's commitment to democracy, especially after they forced through a non-consensual constitution that was boycotted by secularists, and after they started using some of the same repressive techniques of the [Hosni] Mubarak regime. They feared that the Brotherhood would undermine Egypt as a sovereign nation-state and that it would forcibly Islamise Egyptian society.

Moreover, the Brotherhood's economic management was disastrous. During their rule, growth declined, unemployment and inflation rose, and shortages of key necessities (e.g., fuel) became commonplace, culminating in demonstrations for early presidential elections on June 30, 2013. These are the people who today support General al-Sisi and the new constitution.

## Road Map for the Future

But where is Egypt headed now? There are at least three possible scenarios. First, some observers point to the extreme polarisation in Egyptian society between secularists and Islamists and predict a long period of civil strife and instability similar to that experienced by Algeria after the 1991 elections.

Second possibility is growing nationalist sentiment and the popularity of the military/security establishment. They predict that Egypt can become a military dictatorship reminiscent of Chile under General [Augusto] Pinochet. But one can argue that unlike Algeria in the 1990s, Egyptian Islamists are divided between hard-liners, who insist on returning to the status quo ante of July 2, 2013, and pragmatists, who are willing to give the new order a chance, as well as between those who call for peaceful protest and others who espouse violence. Moreover, it can also be argued that unlike Chile of the 1970s, Egyptian youth have learnt to use 'people power'. They will not tolerate living under a dictatorship, whether religious or military, for an extended period of time.

Therefore, under the third (and more optimistic) scenario, the current transition authorities would complete their road map with the election of a new president and parliament. The new elected leadership would then manage a gradual evolution to full democracy and political and economic inclusion. The process of democratisation may be long, because Egypt has weak democratic institutions and limited experience with democracy. Nevertheless, the authorities will have to take visible and concrete steps towards democracy; otherwise, they may risk yet another Egyptian revolution.

> "A constitution isn't going to fix Egypt's
> myriad problems."

# Egypt's Constitutional Referendum: It's Not About Democracy Anymore

*Dan Murphy*

*Dan Murphy is a journalist and staff writer for the* Christian Science Monitor. *In the following viewpoint, he suggests that Egypt's new constitution is a disaster because it takes the country further away from the democratic ideals that spurred the Arab Spring. Murphy argues that the new constitution fails to address many of the fundamental problems—cronyism, police brutality, economic stagnation—that inspired the 2011 protests of Egyptians that overthrew the government of Hosni Mubarak. Instead, the constitution ushers in a new era of authoritarian rule with the Egyptian military still in control of the country. He observes that the great majority of Egyptians are fine with the move toward military rule because it guarantees that the Muslim Brotherhood will not be able to come to power and fundamentally change the tenor of Egyptian society.*

As you read, consider the following questions:

1. According to Murphy, how many national referendums and elections have been held between February 2011 and January 2014?

2. On what day did the initial protests break out in Egypt, according to the viewpoint?

3. For what have Egyptian police arrested citizens, according to Murphy?

The referendum on Egypt's new constitution is wrapping up, its passage a foregone conclusion. The interim military government and its backers have fostered a martial, nationalistic climate around the vote with a simple message: A "yes" vote is a vote for Egypt; a "no" vote is a vote for terrorism and chaos.

By any standard, the vote today is the least free and fair of the five national referendums and elections held since Egypt's military-backed dictator Hosni Mubarak was pushed from power by mass protests in February 2011. The new constitution won't change the principal issues that led to the uprising—rampant police brutality with no accountability, a sclerotic and corrupt economy dominated by the cronies of those in power—and it appears to pave the way for a restoration of the old manner of government that prevailed before the protests against Mubarak broke out.

Is this a complete disaster? Well, if you believe that democracy is the answer to all of society's ills, then yes. Gen. Abdel Fattah al-Sisi, who leads Egypt's interim military government, is now in pole position to win Egypt's presidency and he's not that different from Mr. Mubarak.

But it also can't be ignored that what's going on in Egypt right now is very popular among Egyptians. How popular is difficult to say—but the mass protests that broke out last June against Egypt's first democratically elected president, Mohamed Morsi, creating the conditions for the military's takeover, were by most accounts even larger than the ones that helped sweep Mubarak from power.

The Egyptian military really is wildly popular within Egyptian society, and fear that Mr. Morsi's Muslim Brotherhood would forcibly Islamicize Egyptian society if left in power is real.

This is the paradox of Egyptian politics at the moment. The country is moving further away from democracy and vast numbers of Egyptians, perhaps even a majority, seem OK with it. The room for political dissent that existed in the aftermath of Mubarak's fall has steadily narrowed, and now Egypt is about as free or unfree as it was before Jan. 25, 2011, when protests broke out. Hundreds of political prisoners are in Egypt's jails, police corruption and brutality (which provided the initial spark for the uprising) are as bad as ever, and a climate of fear has returned.

The constitution isn't really that important, though from the perspective of basic rights it seems to be an improvement over the previous document, which had far more democratic legitimacy. This one curtails the role of Islam in legislation, promises equal social and political rights for men and women, provides more latitude for freedom of speech, and bans discrimination based on religion or belief. (Evan Hill has a nice rundown on the differences between this constitution and the 2012 version.) Like the document from 2012, it retains the military's autonomous powers—including the power to try civilians in military courts.

But the words in a constitution are usually far less important than a country's political constitution, and many constitutions that look good on paper (the current Iraqi one comes to mind) are often simply ignored when they get in leaders' way. Is Egypt about to become a paradise for the rights of women or its Christian minorities because the constitution says so? Will the journalists currently in detention be sprung from the jails after the referendum?

Almost certainly not.

None of this can sweep away the grim turn Egypt's so-called "spring" has taken.

Egyptian police have arrested citizens for the crime of campaigning for a "no" vote on the constitution, political paranoia led to the investigation of a satirical television puppet on charges it supports terrorism, and even a hint of sedition can lead to being thrown in jail. Consider this piece by Max Rodenbeck, where he points out that an Egyptian man's home has been raided multiple times by the police and he now sleeps in the olive groves around his village. Why? A car that looks much like his own was captured in a photograph of a pro–Muslim Brotherhood mob burning down a local police station a few months ago. Rodenbeck writes:

> Apparently unconvinced by protests from his family that Mr Y has never had anything to do with the Brothers, officers of the law keep barging into his house. For his own safety Mr Y has given up driving his taxi. He sleeps in the dense olive groves surrounding the village, only occasionally slipping home. He says he would like to give himself up and prove his innocence, but fears he will be dragged off to prison. That is what has happened to several other alleged Muslim Brothers in the village, while the former local Brotherhood MP has fled to Sudan. Not knowing what else to do, Mr Y's family has put up signs affirming that they, too, will proudly vote YES.

Many Egyptians came to believe that straight-up democracy was destined to empower the Muslim Brotherhood, the country's most focused and organized political group, and have supported efforts to prevent that from happening. Since the military came to power, the Brotherhood has been outlawed as a terrorist group (despite having publicly disavowed using political violence to achieve its goals decades ago). The chance of fair and open competition in the political sphere anytime soon is next to none.

Will Egypt be willing to live with that? It certainly seems so for now—though the country's dire economic state and millions living on just a few dollars a day could end up changing that position, again.

A constitution isn't going to fix Egypt's myriad problems. Whether the country's incoming leaders, with the certain to be large influence of the military, will be able to remains to be seen.

If recent history is anything to go by, the outlook is not good.

VIEWPOINT 8

*"Crucially, there is no sign that approval of this new constitution has made, or will make, any positive difference to the country's myriad and chronic problems."*

# Egypt's Constitutional Referendum Has Solved Nothing

*Sharif Nashashibi*

*Sharif Nashashibi is a journalist and cofounder of Arab Media Watch. In the following viewpoint, he suggests that the approval of Egypt's new constitution in January 2014 was "farcical": only a small percentage even knew what was in the document; it was illegal to campaign against it; and voter participation was low. Nashashibi argues that Egyptians who went to the polls overwhelmingly voted for the constitution as a symbolic vote of support for the military regime and to reject the failed leadership of the Muslim Brotherhood. He contends that the new constitution will exacerbate the existing problems in Egypt because it enhances the power of the military. He predicts that giving more power to the military will lead to more political repression and economic stagnation in Egypt.*

As you read, consider the following questions:

1. According to the author, what percentage of Egyptians had read the 2014 constitution before the referendum?

2. How many Egyptians does the author estimate live outside of the country?

3. According to a Baseera poll in December 2013, what percentage of Egyptians rated the government's performance as good?

January's referendum on Egypt's new constitution was not actually about the constitution. Only 5 percent of people had read it prior to the vote, according to the independent Egyptian Center for Public Opinion Research (Baseera), which described this statistic as "remarkable." For most of those who turned out, "the details were irrelevant," wrote Richard Spencer, the *Daily Telegraph*'s Cairo-based Middle East correspondent.

Rather, the referendum was a test of legitimacy and public support for the country's military-backed authorities, and for their ousting in July last year of former president Mohamed Morsi. Their performance was woefully lacking before the constitution was even drafted.

Critics of Morsi's constitution were justified in arguing that the drafting process was not inclusive, and was dominated by Islamists. Its replacement suffered from the same problem in reverse: the 50-member drafting committee included only two Islamists, neither of them from the Muslim Brotherhood, Egypt's largest opposition group. Granted it would have refused to take part, but it said it was never invited to do so anyway.

## 'Closing Democratic Space'

The run-up to the referendum can only be described as farcical. The authorities, their financial backers and a pliant media pumped money, airtime and column space towards a yes vote.

Campaigning for a no vote or a boycott, on the other hand, was all but impossible, with the arrest, beating and prosecution of those who did so, the closure of opposition and even independent media, and the banning of the Brotherhood as a 'terrorist' group.

Though the organization would have boycotted the referendum anyway, state intimidation was cited by other parties as the reason they were joining the boycott. These included the Strong Egypt Party and the April 6 Youth Movement, both of which opposed Morsi's constitution.

Democracy International, which according to the *Financial Times* "fielded the most robust international monitoring operation," expressed "serious concerns" about the political environment preceding the latest vote. "There was no real opportunity ... to dissent," said the Washington-based consultancy. "This constrained campaign environment made a robust debate on the substance and merits of the constitution impossible."

Transparency International, which also sent observers for the referendum, condemned "repression by state authorities" prior to the vote. The government "harassed, arrested, and prosecuted peaceful critics, closing democratic space to promote views and debate before the referendum," said the Berlin-based anti-corruption organization.

The U.S.-based Carter Center, which observed the previous constitutional vote, said it was "deeply concerned" by the "narrowed political space surrounding the upcoming referendum." It said it would not field observers this time because "the late release of regulations for accreditation of witnesses" meant that the center would be unable to do its job properly.

The result was "the least free and fair of the five national referendums and elections held since Egypt's military-backed dictator Hosni Mubarak was pushed from power by mass protests in February 2011," wrote *Christian Science Monitor* correspondent Dan Murphy. For all Morsi's faults—and he had many—at least there was a vigorous campaign against his constitution, by opposition groups that were not outlawed.

The authorities failed to prevent violence during the two-day vote, despite the deployment of tens of thousands of soldiers. Those soldiers were also the cause of much of that violence, with demonstrators killed, injured, beaten or dispersed, and hundreds arrested.

## Turnout

Although Morsi's constitution passed with some 64 percent of votes, its critics argued with some justification that the constitution still lacked sufficient legitimacy because of the low turnout of just 33 percent. Even though the new constitution garnered support from some 98 percent of those who voted—hardly surprising given the boycott and the crackdown on a no vote—it managed only a slightly higher turnout of 38.6 percent.

Furthermore, Al Jazeera English reported that less than 682,000 Egyptian expatriates registered to vote on the election committee's website, out of anywhere between 2.7 million and 8 million Egyptians live outside the country.

Election commission head Nabil Salib's description of the vote as an "unrivalled success" with "unprecedented turnout" is laughable. Turnout was dismal even by the standards of the constitution-drafting committee, which—according to its head Amr Moussa—was hoping for a turnout of 75 percent. The actual figure was almost half that. Moussa himself said he expected a "huge" and "unprecedented" turnout—38.6 percent qualifies as neither.

Turnout was particularly lacking given three important factors. Firstly, the government had said participation was a patriotic duty. Secondly, the Salafist Al-Nour Party—which won the second-largest number of seats in the last parliamentary elections, after the Brotherhood—supported the new constitution.

Thirdly, army chief Abdel Fattah al-Sisi—who is widely viewed in almost messianic terms—had reportedly hinted that he would consider a high turnout (as well as a strong yes vote) as a mandate to run for president later this year.

The low turnout can be interpreted as a victory for the boycott movement, which involved dozens of groups and political parties. Some see it rather as a sign of public apathy—this may well be a contributing factor.

However, it is countered by a Baseera poll in December, in which only 20 percent of Egyptians rated the government's performance as good. "Egyptians' sentiments toward the government . . . are entirely negative," said Magued Osman, CEO and managing director of Baseera.

A breakdown of the turnout figure paints an even bleaker picture. "Across much of Egypt's rural, impoverished south barely a quarter of voters bothered to show up this time, and only 16 percent in the religiously conservative coastal province of Mersa Matruh. Nationwide, the figure for voters under the age of 30 was barely 20 percent," read an editorial in the *Economist*.

"Such discrepancies reflect not only the hardening of a dangerous polarisation between Islamists and their foes, but widespread disgruntlement among Egypt's youth," the editorial added. "A generation of young Egyptians felt briefly and giddily empowered by the 2011 revolution. They now sense that the 'wall of fear' they had demolished is being rebuilt around them, brick by brick."

## Bleak Prospects

Just as Morsi's constitution exacerbated national divisions while promising the opposite, the same is true of its replacement. It has simply entrenched the idea of three increasingly irreconcilable Egypts: that which supports Sisi and the military, that which backs Morsi and the Brotherhood, and that which opposes both.

# Egypt's Constitutional Referendum

Egypt's turbulent experiment in participatory democracy the last three years [2011–2014] has reminded us all that it's not one vote that determines a democracy, it's all the steps that follow. It's a challenging transition that demands compromise, vigilance, and constant tending. The draft Egyptian constitution passed a public referendum this week [January 2014], but it's what comes next that will shape Egypt's political, economic and social framework for generations.

As Egypt's transition proceeds, the United States urges the interim Egyptian government to fully implement those rights and freedoms that are guaranteed in the new constitution for the benefit of the Egyptian people, and to take steps towards reconciliation.

The brave Egyptians who stood vigil in Tahrir Square did not risk their lives in a revolution to see its historic potential squandered in the transition. They've weathered ups and downs, disappointment and setbacks in the years that followed, and they're still searching for the promise of that revolution. They still know that the path forward to an inclusive, tolerant, and civilian-led democracy will require Egypt's political leaders to make difficult compromises and seek a broad consensus on many divisive issues.

Democracy is more than any one referendum or election. It is about equal rights and protections under the law for all Egyptians, regardless of their gender, faith, ethnicity, or political affiliation.

*John Kerry,*
*"Egypt's Constitutional Referendum,"*
*US Department of State, January 18, 2014.*

This process will continue with the almost-certain scenario of a military figure (Sisi) as the next president, and an ever-widening clampdown on dissent. Mubarak must be getting a strong and satisfying sense of déjà vu.

Crucially, there is no sign that approval of this new constitution has made, or will make, any positive difference to the country's myriad and chronic problems. If anything, deadly violence is worsening, wholesale disenfranchisement is becoming more entrenched, human rights are being trampled on by a fully resurgent police state, and the economy remains on life support.

"Egypt has witnessed a series of damaging blows to human rights and state violence on an unprecedented scale" since Morsi's ouster, Hassiba Hadj Sahraoui, Middle East and North Africa deputy director at Amnesty International, said in a report published in January. Egypt, where "the current state of human rights is abysmal," is "headed firmly down the path towards further repression and confrontation."

Indeed, the new constitution enhances even further the power and impunity of the military, whose political and economic influence was already pervasive, even during Egypt's short-lived period of civilian democratic rule. Amnesty's secretary general Salil Shetty added in a subsequent report that "only one narrative is acceptable in Egypt today—that which is sanctioned by the Egyptian authorities."

Murphy concludes that "the words in a constitution are usually far less important than a country's political constitution, and many constitutions that look good on paper (the current Iraqi one comes to mind) are often simply ignored when they get in leaders' way.

"Is Egypt about to become a paradise for the rights of women or its Christian minorities because the constitution says so? Will the journalists currently in detention be sprung from the jails after the referendum? Almost certainly not.... If recent history is anything to go by, the outlook is not good."

# Periodical and Internet Sources Bibliography

*The following articles have been selected to supplement the diverse views presented in this chapter.*

| | |
|---|---|
| *America* | "Despite Terror Strikes in Cairo, New Constitution Offers Hope," February 10, 2014. |
| Gregg Carlstrom | "What's in Egypt's Proposed New Constitution?," Al Jazeera, January 14, 2014. |
| William Dermody and Sarah Lynch | "The Egypt Semantics Debate: Is It a Coup? A Civil War?," *USA Today*, August 16, 2013. |
| Robert Fisk | "When Is a Military Coup not a Military Coup? When It Happens in Egypt, Apparently," *Independent* (UK), July 4, 2013. |
| Agustino Fontevecchia | "Coup D'Etat in Egypt: Military Removes President Morsi and Suspends the Constitution," *Forbes*, July 3, 2013. |
| Yahia Hamed | "Egypt's Coup Has Plunged the Country into Catastrophe," *Guardian*, March 16, 2014. |
| Jonathan Marcus | "Egypt Turmoil: Coup or No Coup?," BBC News, July 4, 2013. |
| Andrew C. McCarthy | "Sharia After Morsi: Egypt Revolted Against Inept Governance, Not Islamic Supremacism," *National Review Online*, August 5, 2013. |
| Reza Sayah and Mohammed Tawfeeq | "Egypt Passes a New Constitution," CNN, January 18, 2014. |
| Lee Smith | "No More Morsi: A Coup in Ungovernable Egypt," *Weekly Standard*, July 22, 2013. |
| Ben Wedeman, Reza Sayah, and Matt Smith | "Coup Topples Egypt's Morsy; Deposed President Under 'House Arrest,'" CNN, July 4, 2013. |

# CHAPTER 2

# What Is the Impact of Recent Political and Social Upheaval in Egypt?

# Chapter Preface

On July 3, 2013, media outlets across the world reported the gang rape of a twenty-two-year-old Dutch journalist by five men during antigovernment protests in Tahrir Square, an area in Cairo that has been the location of numerous political protests over the Egypt's modern history. After the attack, the young woman was taken to the hospital by authorities and underwent surgery to address horrific injuries she sustained as a result.

The attack on the Dutch journalist follows other shocking cases of sexual violence against foreign female journalists in Egypt. In one well-publicized incident, the French journalist Sonia Dridi was attacked and groped by a group of men while filming a report for France 24 in Tahrir Square. On February 11, 2011, South African journalist Lara Logan was beaten and sexually assaulted by a large group of men after filming a report for American television about the celebration over the resignation of former Egyptian president Hosni Mubarak. After being dragged along the square, she was rescued by a group of female and male protesters. In the cases of Dridi and Logan, not one of the attackers was prosecuted.

These shocking crimes generated worldwide media coverage. Unfortunately, these are not isolated incidents. There has been a long history of sexual assault in Tahrir Square since the onset of the Egyptian revolution in 2011. The victims of these horrific crimes are women—grandmothers, housewives, students, teenagers—courageous enough to go out and protest Egypt's political situation. It is estimated that thousands of these women have been groped, beaten, molested, and gang-raped during protests. Operation Anti Sexual Harassment (OpAntiSH), a volunteer group formed to protect female protesters in Tahrir Square, reports that forty-six cases of sexual assault occurred on one day, June 30, 2013. The next day, seventeen more were reported.

Human Rights Watch reports that many of the attacks seem to follow a similar pattern. "Typically a handful of young men at demonstrations single out a woman and encircle her, separating her from her friends," the organization states. "During the attacks—which have lasted from a few minutes to more than an hour—the number of attackers increases and they grope the woman's body and try to remove her clothing. The attackers often try to drag the woman to a different location while continuing to attack her. In some cases, the attackers have assaulted other women and activists with sticks and knives for trying to rescue the victims. Survivors and witnesses told Human Rights Watch that some of the men claiming to help the women during the attacks were in fact taking part, further disorienting victims, who could not assess who was in fact assisting them," Human Rights Watch explained.

For many, the frequent violence against female protesters and journalists in Tahrir Square was part of a larger attempt to intimidate women into staying home and denying them participation in Egyptian civic life. To many observers, the election of Mohamed Morsi and the Muslim Brotherhood signaled a trend toward a conservative Islamist ideology, which dictates that women stay out of the public square and focus on their roles as wife and mother. One conservative Islamic cleric even stated in an online video that the rape of female protesters in Tahrir Square was justified.

The unsettling issue of the escalating rates of sexual violence and harassment of women is one of the subjects considered in the following chapter, which discusses the impact of recent political and social upheaval in Egypt.

> "Over the past few months, thousands of [Muslim] Brotherhood members and [Mohamed] Morsi supporters have been rounded up and thrown in prison."

# Civil Liberties Are Being Violated in Egypt

## Sharif Abdel Kouddous

*Sharif Abdel Kouddous is a journalist and fellow at the Nation Institute. In the following viewpoint, he reports on a recent visit to Abu Zaabal prison outside of Cairo, where thousands of prisoners are housed. Many of them are political prisoners—members of the Muslim Brotherhood, critics of the military regime, protest leaders—or journalists arrested for writing articles supportive of the regime of Mohamed Morsi, the former president and a member of the Muslim Brotherhood. Kouddous maintains that security forces have also begun rounding up non-Islamist activists, students, bloggers, and even bystanders. Prisoners are routinely beaten and tortured. Kouddous further notes that recent activities to protest the widespread violation of civil rights have ended in beatings and mass killings, as the military regime has intensified its efforts to quell dissent on college campuses and in major cities.*

As you read, consider the following questions:

1. According to the author, how many people attending sit-ins in Cairo and Giza on August 14, 2013, were killed by security forces?

2. What is drawn on the walls of Abu Zaabal prison, according to Kouddous?

3. What two prominent bloggers have been arrested in recent months and accused of violating a new anti-protest law?

The Abu Zaabal prison complex lies some twenty miles northeast of Cairo, where the dense urban cacophony of the capital quickly gives way to rolling fields, rubbish-strewn canals and small clusters of hastily built red brick buildings. Outside the main gate—a pair of large metal doors flanked by Pharaonic-themed columns—sit four army tanks, their long snouts pointed up and out.

## Prison Life

Gehad Khaled, a 20-year-old with an easy laugh and youthful intensity, has been coming to Abu Zaabal on a regular basis for nearly four months to visit her imprisoned husband. Abdullah al-Shamy was among hundreds rounded up on August 14 [2013], the day security forces violently stormed two sit-ins in Cairo and Giza that formed the epicenter of support for the deposed president, Mohamed Morsi, leaving up to 1,000 people dead.

Abdullah was at the Rabaa Al-Adawiya sit-in for work. As a correspondent for the satellite news channel Al Jazeera, the 25-year-old journalist had been stationed at the pro-Morsi encampment for six weeks, becoming a familiar face to the channel's viewers in one of the summer's biggest international news stories.

Gehad would visit Abdullah at the sit-in, where he was working around the clock. The two had been married in September 2012, though Abdullah spent little time at home because of regular deployments to countries like Mali, Libya, Ghana and Turkey for Al Jazeera. "The longest period we spent together since we were married was in Rabaa," she says with a smile.

Now, Gehad sees Abdullah just once every two weeks inside Abu Zaabal, waiting hours each time for a fifteen-minute visit. She brings him food, water, clothes, newspapers, books, toiletries and other necessities to alleviate the austere conditions inside Egypt's jails.

The prison waiting room is bustling with other families carrying plastic bags and suitcases of supplies. Children scamper around their parents, women carry babies. Over the past few months, thousands of [Muslim] Brotherhood members and Morsi supporters have been rounded up and thrown in prison. More than 700 of those arrested in the August 14 raid on Rabaa were imprisoned at Abu Zaabal, and the walls of the waiting room bear the signs of the political divisions that have torn Egypt apart.

## Political Prisoners

Drawings of a hand holding up four fingers, a symbol for Rabaa (Arabic for "four"), are scrawled in felt pen alongside slogans such as "Down with military rule" and "CC the killer," in reference to army chief Abdel Fattah al-Sisi, who deposed Morsi on July 3. Some of the graffiti has been angrily crossed out by family members of prisoners convicted of regular crimes who oppose the Brotherhood.

Similar divisions exist within Gehad's own family. Her father is a member of the Muslim Brotherhood and a staunch supporter of Morsi, yet Gehad, who has been protesting the regime since 2008, says she doesn't support the group and accuses them of abandoning the revolution. In what has become an increasingly common phenomenon in Egyptian society, the political cleavages within her family often spilled over into heated disputes, compelling her to refrain from discussing politics with her parents and siblings.

Despite her misgivings about the Brotherhood, Gehad spent a lot of time in the pro-Morsi Rabaa sit-in, not just to see her husband but to be a part of the protest. "We have been standing against the military since 2011, and we still are now," she explains. "We didn't change our position, the Brotherhood did. Now they stand against the military too. We are continuing, and they have joined us." Her attitude is not shared by other revolutionary activists who view the Brotherhood not just as political opportunists but as a separate wing of the counterrevolution. These activists point to abuses the Brotherhood committed during their time in power as justification for refusing to join even a tactical alliance with them against the military after the coup.

Abdullah's younger brother, 23-year-old Mosa'ab, sits next to Gehad in the waiting room. Mosa'ab also spent a significant amount of time in Rabaa, but only in his capacity as a journalist, not as a protester. A talented and intrepid freelance photographer, one of his photographs, from a police attack on the sit-in on July 27 that left dozens dead, was selected as one of *Time* magazine's top ten photos of 2013.

## Political Divisions

Similar divisions plague the al-Shamy family as well. Mosa'ab says his father, a Brotherhood member, and his eldest brother, Anas, are often a united front arguing vociferously against him, Abdullah and his younger brother, all of whom were more critical of the Brotherhood and Morsi. "It wasn't pleasant," Mosa'ab says.

On August 14, the day of the police raids, Mosa'ab was in frequent phone contact with Abdullah as they both covered the carnage unfolding in Rabaa. Their youngest brother, 19-

year-old Mohammed, a photographer working for the Turkish news agency Anadolu, was there as well. Mosa'ab and Mohammed left together in the afternoon, not long before security forces had completely moved in and cleared the sit-in.

By nightfall, Mosa'ab found out that Abdullah had been detained, arrested by security forces as he was walking out of Rabaa with Gehad. Nearly four months later, he remains imprisoned, and there have been no significant developments pointing toward his release. Like thousands of protesters arrested over the past few months, he is accused of inciting violence, disturbing the peace and destroying public property.

"I'm more afraid now," Mosa'ab says of continuing his work as a photojournalist in Egypt. "I think about it 1,000 times over before I go out to cover something."

## Abdullah

Abdullah has spent the past four months struggling to endure the monotony of prison life.

"People should appreciate every moment they live in freedom," he says in an interview from jail. "I never thought I could stay this long here. The worst thing is that every day is like the other. You wake up with nothing to do."

He spends his days reading, writing and speaking to other prisoners. He shares a cell with sixty-six other men, in a room approximately forty square meters. There are no beds; prisoners sleep on the floor, with blankets provided by their families. For the first eight weeks, hardly any water was provided, and prisoners had to structure an equitable sharing system in order to shower. The cell is open for an hour a day, when prisoners can walk around the building but are not allowed outside.

Ever the journalist, Abdullah has spent much of his time in prison interviewing all of his fellow detainees and documenting their cases. He plans to write a book once he is released. He says those imprisoned with him include Islamists spanning different ideologies as well as street vendors, minors and even one man detained simply for standing near police on the day of the Rabaa raid who says he is staunchly opposed to Morsi, voted for his rival in the presidential election and took part in the anti-Morsi protest on June 30 and the pro-military one on July 26.

## The Arrest

Like many other prisoners, the worst abuse Abdullah suffered occurred when he was first detained. Officers arrested him as he was walking out of Rabaa with Gehad past a security checkpoint. They asked for his ID, but all he had was his passport, which was filled with entry stamps from the countries across Africa where he had been deployed for Al Jazeera. "They considered me a spy," he says. "They thought I was a big catch."

He was taken to the nearby Cairo stadium, where prisoners were being mistreated and harassed by the police. The next morning he was transferred with several dozen others to a police station, where they were greeted by the notorious "welcome party"—a common practice of forcing incoming detainees to run through a gantlet of waiting soldiers, who beat and whip them with sticks and belts. Once inside, police stole money, watches and IDs from the prisoners while continuing to beat and humiliate them, Abdullah says.

All of them were eventually transferred to Abu Zaabal, where they have remained ever since, relying on regular supplies of food, water and other essentials from relatives, as is customary in Egypt's crippled prison system.

"I do have hope," he says. "But sometimes I feel down because my wife has to endure this in the beginning of our marriage. I am lucky she is a very strong lady and is supporting me when I should be supporting her."

## Twenty-Seven Countries Address Human Rights Situation in Egypt

Three years have passed since Egyptians from all walks of life rose against a repressive government calling for freedom, human dignity, social justice and a better economy. Like many, we have been following the developments ever since. The outcome is not only important to the Egyptian people but also to the region and the international community. We share the high commissioner's concern about the escalating violence and her call on all sides to renounce the use of violence. Further, we strongly condemn the reprehensible terrorist attacks in Sinai and elsewhere.

We express concern about the restrictions on the rights to peaceful assembly, expression and association, and about the disproportionate use of lethal force by security forces against demonstrators which resulted in large numbers of deaths and injuries. Security forces have a duty to respect the right to peaceful assembly and should operate in line with the state's international human rights obligations and commitments relevant to the use of force, even when faced with persistent security challenges.

*"Denmark and 26 Other Countries Address Human Rights Situation in Egypt at HRC25," Permanent Mission of Denmark to the United Nations in Geneva, March 7, 2014.*

## The Politics of Egyptian Journalism

Abdullah has received scant backing for his plight from other journalists in Egypt outside of his friends. The Journalists Syndicate has not taken up his case, and calls for his release are largely absent in the local press. "Some Egyptian journalists are very happy about it, including people that we know," says his brother Mosa'ab. "They think he deserves it."

Abdullah's network, Al Jazeera, has long been criticized as being heavily biased in favor of the Muslim Brotherhood and the Morsi government's agenda. After Morsi's ouster, authorities raided the offices of Al Jazeera's local affiliate in Egypt and briefly detained its staff. In September, a Cairo court ordered the channel and three other stations to stop broadcasting, saying in its ruling that they "hurt national security."

Yet the criticism did not just come from the military-backed government. Even Mosa'ab would argue with Abdullah over the channel's coverage. "I would criticize Al Jazeera and tell him about my reservations and tell him to keep his integrity," Mosa'ab says. "He always took the criticism well but did what he believed."

"Every channel is biased or has its agenda, no channel is completely neutral," Abdullah says. "I always challenge people to point to something I said on air, and I will face any allegations," he says. "Our job is to help the weak. But unfortunately, in Egypt most journalists stand with those in power, either Mubarak or the Supreme Council of the Armed Forces or Sisi."

In the deepening polarization following Morsi's overthrow, many pundits on private media outlets have voiced complete support for the military, adopting its language of a "war on terror" and vilifying Al Jazeera and demonizing all Islamists as violent extremists unfit for political life.

"The polarization was a big divide that resulted in a lack of empathy and solidarity between journalists," says Sherif Mansour, the Middle East and North Africa coordinator for the Committee to Protect Journalists. "This is one of the main reasons we've seen these attacks on journalists increase but also go unpunished." Seven journalists, including Abdullah, are currently imprisoned in Egypt, according to Mansour, while dozens of others have been briefly detained.

## Growing Political Oppression

Meanwhile, after months of a vicious crackdown targeting the Muslim Brotherhood and Morsi supporters, the Interior Ministry has turned its attention to the activist community that first launched and sustained the revolution. Prominent figures, like blogger Alaa Abd El Fattah and Ahmed Douma, have been arrested in the middle of the night at their homes and accused of violating a draconian new anti-protest law. Dozens of non-Islamist protesters—among them some of the country's most notable female activists—have been detained during peaceful demonstrations and beaten and abused while in police custody. And security forces have tried to quell a growing firestorm of protest and dissent on university campuses with brute force, killing at least one student and arresting scores in mass sweeps.

"I don't think the people who stood against Morsi wanted this," Abdullah says. "The way things are going, nothing is going to change in Egypt."

> *"Sexual assaults at protests, where women have been groped, stripped and even raped, have risen both in number and intensity in the past year, reaching a peak on the uprising's anniversary."*

# Sexual Harassment of and Violence Against Women Are on the Rise

*Brian Rohan*

*Brian Rohan is a journalist for the Associated Press. In the following viewpoint, he reports that Egyptian women and international human rights groups are increasingly concerned about the rise in sexual assaults against women, especially female protesters. Rohan notes that although the harassment of women has long been a problem in Egypt, the attacks have become more violent and frequent. Several hard-line conservative figures, including a prominent Islamic cleric, have blamed women for the rise in violent sexual attacks, stating that by going to protests they should expect to be raped. The backlash against these remarks has been strong, with women in Egypt and neighboring countries organizing protests and strategy sessions to formulate a plan of action. A number of women have formed self-defense*

*groups, training to protect themselves from male violence at pro-*
*tests and in their daily lives. Rohan says there has also been a*
*concerted effort to raise awareness of the problem among Egyp-*
*tian men and women.*

As you read, consider the following questions:

1. According to Rohan, how many women were sexually assaulted at demonstrations in Cairo on January 25, 2013?

2. What did conservative politician Adel Afify say about the culpability of female protesters in Egypt?

3. According to the viewpoint, what American official criticized the Egyptian criminal justice system for failing to effectively address the problem of violence against women?

Egyptian women are growing increasingly angry and militant as they deal with one of the unintended consequences of the Arab Spring: an epidemic of sexual assault that law enforcement has failed to contain.

The backlash, which includes self-defense courses for women and even threats of violent retaliation, is fueled by ultraconservative Islamists who suggest that women invite assault by attending antigovernment protests where they mix with men.

At marches against sexual harassment in Cairo, women have brandished kitchen knives in the air. Stenciled drawings on building walls depict girls fighting off men with swords. Signs threaten to "cut off the hand" of attackers.

The reaction comes at a particularly heated moment. While the latest wave of demonstrations against President Mohamed Morsi's rule has cooled in recent days, large protests have grown increasingly violent.

A hard-core minority of demonstrators has vowed to take on the government, and police have responded with force.

About 70 people have been killed in clashes with security forces since Jan. 25 [2013], the second anniversary of the revolt that deposed longtime autocrat Hosni Mubarak.

## A Longtime Problem

Harassment has long been a problem in this patriarchal society, and attacks against female demonstrators have occurred under the democratically elected Morsi, the military council that ruled before him and Mubarak, who governed the Arab world's most populous country for nearly three decades.

The new element, however, is the increasingly sexual nature of the violence.

Sexual assaults at protests, where women have been groped, stripped and even raped, have risen both in number and intensity in the past year, reaching a peak on the uprising's anniversary.

On that day alone, activists reported two dozen cases of assaults against women at demonstrations in and around Cairo's central Tahrir Square, one of which involved the rape of a 19-year-old. The United Nations responded by urging the government to take action.

Activists say the attacks are organized by opponents of the demonstrations, who aim to make protests seem less representative by removing women from the scene. To date, no specific groups have been charged.

Hard-line Islamists have seized on the issue to propose their own solution: limit female protesters to designated areas.

## Blaming Women

On Monday [February 11, 2013], members of the human rights commission of the Islamist-dominated legislative assembly criticized women for rallying among men and in areas considered unsafe.

While they urged passage of a new law to regulate demonstrations and facilitate police protection, one prominent member said that women should not go to protests.

"Sometimes, the girl herself is fully responsible for rape because she puts herself in this situation," lawmaker Adel Afify said in comments carried by several Egyptian newspapers.

The remarks followed a video posted last week by a hardline cleric, who said women headed to protests were "crusaders" and "devils," who were "going there to get raped." The cleric, [Ahmed] Mohammed Abdullah, and Afify are both members of the ultraconservative Salafi movement.

## The Backlash

Women's rights groups were infuriated, denouncing the comments in demonstrations in Egypt and elsewhere Tuesday. A Beirut-based online movement, the Uprising of Women in the Arab World, called for worldwide protests in front of Egyptian embassies, posting photos of demonstrations from a string of countries on their Facebook page.

On the same day in Egypt, Michael Posner, the U.S. assistant secretary of state for democracy, human rights and labor, criticized what he said was the failure of the country's criminal justice system to identify and bring to justice perpetrators "involved in an alarming number of rapes and other acts of violence against women."

In meetings with Egyptian officials, including the foreign and justice ministers, the nation's top cleric and a presidential adviser, Posner said he expressed Washington's concern that the rights of women are not being prioritized alongside other key issues such as transparency, rule of law and building a better climate for civil society.

## Protecting Female Protesters

Last weekend in the leafy Cairo neighborhood of Maadi, dozens of women were learning how to fight back. They attended a self-defense course on how to escape an attacker by striking

## Violence Against Women

Violence against women is a problem that cuts across geographic, racial, and economic boundaries. The wealthy and the poor, residents of developed and developing nations, Muslims, Hindus, Christians, Jews—all witness the effects of violence against women.

Egypt witnessed an upsurge in violence directed against women in the second half of 2013, amid ongoing political instability. Conditions for women, which were highly restricted under Egypt's longtime leader Hosni Mubarak (1928–), worsened under the military and Muslim Brotherhood–led governments that followed Mubarak's ouster in the 2011 revolution. Dozens of women participating in political protests in Cairo's Tahrir Square in 2013 were attacked by mobs, sexually assaulted, or raped. A Thomson Reuters Foundation poll released in November ranked Egypt last among twenty-two Arab nations for women's rights. Earlier in the year, the UN [United Nations] reported that more than 99 percent of Egyptian women had been subject to some form of sexual harassment.

*"Violence Against Women,"*
*Global Issues in Context Online Collection.*
*Detroit, MI: Gale, 2014.*

at weak points on the neck and face. The carrying of knives, after proper training, was presented as a personal choice, although one that could carry heavy consequences for both defender and attacker.

"We're facing daily sexual harassment in the streets, and we aim to defend ourselves," said Menna Essam, a 26-year-old Internet marketer. Like most women taking the course, she said she had experienced physical harassment where self-defense techniques would have been useful.

"Of course I faced it growing up. . . . The first time I was maybe 10 or 11 years old. Someone followed me on the way home and grabbed me. At the time, I didn't even know what harassment was," she said.

The free course was organized by Tahrir Bodyguard, one of several groups that have emerged to protect female demonstrators at street protests. The courses aim above all to boost women's confidence and deter what organizers call daily harassment.

## Fighting Back

Women have also been coming forward to talk about attacks, defying long-held taboos in the conservative country.

One who spoke to private Egyptian television channels at length last week, Yasmine Al-Baramawy, described how a gang of men assaulted her for more than an hour near Tahrir Square, dragging her through the streets, tearing off her shirt and cutting her pants.

On Monday, Egypt's National Council of Women also entered the debate, adopting activists' view that the attacks are organized.

In a statement, the council said it "condemned the abuses suffered by Egyptian women from harassment and rape in Tahrir Square recently, which is systematic and carried out by organized groups to force women not to participate and express their views."

Images promoting Tuesday's global protest—from Arab countries and elsewhere—have been among the most militant. The uprising movement, for example, has turned a photo of a veiled woman brandishing a knife at a Cairo protest last week into a poster.

Another image featured on the page shows the late Egyptian singer Umm Kulthum, an iconic figure in the nation's struggle against Israel following the 1967 Middle East war. She is seen holding a superimposed kitchen knife, with a printed lyric from one of her most famous songs that says: "Patience has limits!"

"*The problem, in short, is that despite the likes of the US president, Barack Obama, or the great and the good of the EU, seemingly championing the striving for freedom evident during the Arab Spring, as soon as the Egyptian people began to realise that freedom, and voted for what were perceived to be the wrong guys . . . the cheerleading from the West ceased.*"

# Egypt's Military Coup Is Undoing the Gains of the Arab Spring

*Tim Black*

*Tim Black is the deputy editor at* Spiked. *In the following viewpoint, he classifies the ouster of democratically elected Egyptian president Mohamed Morsi in July 2013 by the military as a coup. Black reports that since the military takeover, the Islamist Muslim Brotherhood has been banned; pro-Morsi protesters have been arrested, beaten, and jailed; free speech and freedom of the press have been further limited; and Morsi himself has been arrested on trumped-up charges and jailed. Western governments*

*have largely condoned the move and have refrained from criti-
cizing the military government, led by strongman General Abdel
Fattah al-Sisi. Black argues that Western leaders and media supporters who were onetime champions of the Arab Spring care
nothing about freedom and democracy and only about their own
agenda.*

As you read, consider the following questions:

1. According to Black, what percentage of Egyptians voted
   for Mohamed Morsi in the 2012 presidential election?

2. In the January 2014 constitutional referendum, what
   percentage of voters approved of the new constitution?

3. What did *New York Times* columnist David Brooks write
   about the election of Mohamed Morsi in 2012, according to the viewpoint?

What has happened in Egypt over the past seven months
ought to chill the democratic blood. It ought to command the attention of anyone who claims to care about defending freedom.

Think back to 3 July 2013: the Egyptian military, under
the leadership of General Abdel Fattah al-Sisi, deposed the
Egyptian president, Mohamed Morsi. Despite the reluctance of
Western politicians to use the phrase at the time, this was a
coup d'état.

Morsi, a leading member of the conservative Muslim
Brotherhood and chairman of its political wing, the Freedom
and Justice Party, had become, just over a year earlier, Egypt's
first-ever democratically elected head of state, winning 52 per
cent of the vote. This ought to have been a historical moment
to savour; this ought to have been the time when Egyptians
began finally to enjoy some of the democratic freedom we
have long exercised in the West; this ought to have been the
time to bid an unfond farewell to the years of Hosni Mubarak's

military dictatorship. But in July last year, just like that, it was over: The democratic flame had been extinguished.

## The Military Coup

After a few days of unrest in Cairo's Tahrir Square, during which antigovernment protesters expressed their anger at Morsi's Islamist tendencies and economic inaction, the army, the tanks and the jets moved in, and switched the whole thing off. Over the following weeks, as supporters of Morsi rallied and set up protest camps in and around Cairo, al-Sisi's 'interim' government declared a state of emergency and began a crackdown on the protesters. By the end of August, the beatings and killings served up by the army, alongside the revived, reviled secret police, had enforced some semblance of order.

As the months have passed, General al-Sisi has furnished this naked display of might with the veneer of right. In September, the Cairo Court for Urgent Matters banned the Muslim Brotherhood, the political and religious movement that, just a few months earlier, had formed the basis for Egypt's first-ever democratically elected power; the arrest, torture and killing of Morsi supporters now had a legal sanction. And Morsi himself—alongside many of the Brotherhood's leading figures—was left potentially facing the death penalty on trumped-up charges.

## The New Constitution

And then, in late 2013, al-Sisi published a new constitution for the Egyptian state, drawn up by a 50-strong committee of coup supporters. Unsurprisingly, it preserved the military's privileged position, guaranteeing the secrecy of its budget, permitting it to try civilians in military courts, and stipulating that, for the next eight years, Egypt's defence minister must be approved by the military.

When the new constitution was put to the Egyptian electorate last week [in January 2014] in a referendum, over 98 per cent voted in favour. Given the palpable absence of a 'no' campaign, the outlawing of political opposition, and the deployment of 160,000 soldiers and 200,000 policemen to 'oversee' voting, the fact that al-Sisi won was less a democratic triumph than a *fait accompli*. Indeed, it has since emerged that over 60 per cent of the electorate either didn't vote or refused to vote. Not that al-Sisi seems to care. With his uniformed image adorning everything from cupcakes to pajamas, and his each and every public appearance prompting a carefully managed wave of euphoria from the select throng of supporters, al-Sisi is now said to be considering whether to do what his handpicked public is demanding and stand for president. His opponents, meanwhile, both secular and Muslim Brotherhood, continue to be rounded up and thrown in jail.

## Global Apathy

Yet where is the international outrage? Where are the leaders of the nominally free world issuing sharply worded condemnations of this authoritarian turn? If this was Zimbabwe, with Robert Mugabe beating and rigging his way to near unanimous electoral victories, no doubt Britain's foreign secretary William Hague would be pontificating from on high. If this was Colonel [Muammar] Gaddafi's Libya, no doubt the self-righteous guffawing from the White House would have been audible in Tripoli.

But this is not Libya or Zimbabwe or one of those other easy stages for Western political posturing. This is Egypt, a place where the hypocrisy and double standards of Western leaders and the political punditariat lay so shamelessly exposed last summer. The problem, in short, is that despite the likes of the US president, Barack Obama, or the great and the good of the EU, seemingly championing the striving for freedom evident during the Arab Spring, as soon as the Egyptian people began to realise that freedom, and voted for what were perceived to be the wrong guys, the less-than-PC Muslim

Brotherhood, the cheerleading from the West ceased. In its place was a willingness to approve the overthrowing of a democratically elected government on the basis that the Egyptian people had proved their immaturity, their inability to exercise their democratic rights correctly.

Little wonder, then, that the military coup was given such prominent international backing right from the start: It was seen as a necessary correction to a democratic error, a righting of the Egyptian people's mistake. The US secretary of state, John Kerry, even went so far as to call General al-Sisi's military government a regime for 'restoring democracy'. And Baroness Ashton [Catherine Ashton], the EU's foreign affairs chief, spent much of last year meeting with al-Sisi and praising him for continuing on the 'journey [towards] a stable, prosperous and democratic Egypt'.

## 'Road Map' to Democracy

That support, that moral bolstering of al-Sisi's military dictatorship, has continued throughout the crackdown, throughout the transformation of Egypt into something that looks very much like an autocracy—indeed, something that looks very much like Mubarak's regime. So in November, amid the arrests and the passing of oppressive anti-protest laws, Kerry said that the 'road map' to democracy was 'being carried out to the best of our perception'. There are none so blind, it seems, as those who see only what they want. Last week, speaking of a referendum so biased that even North Korea's erstwhile dictator Kim Jong-il would have blushed, Kerry continued in his mission to twist reality in accordance with his prejudices: '[General al-Sisi's] government has committed repeatedly to a transition process that expands democratic rights and leads to a civilian-led, inclusive government through free and fair elections.' While Kerry was tying himself in knots, Ashton seemed content to praise 'the Egyptian people and the

## Arab Spring

The term "Arab Spring" is used by the Western media to refer to a series of events in North Africa and the Middle East that began in late 2010, after a street vendor in Tunisia set himself on fire in front of a municipal building to protest his living conditions and the Tunisian government. His public act of protest sparked a full-blown rebellion in Tunisia, which then touched off protests and revolutions throughout the Arab world. More than a dozen Arab nations saw sweeping grassroots movements that resulted in political changes. In some countries, these changes were achieved through nonviolent protests; however, in others, such protests turned to violent revolution. In Egypt, Libya, Tunisia, and Yemen, protesters forced the replacements of dictatorial governments with democratic systems. In other countries, the waves of protests forced governments to offer political reforms or to start dialogues about political change. Some of these movements have proven more successful than others, and the political future of many Arab nations remains uncertain, but the power and importance of this unprecedented pro-democracy movement is beyond question.

*"Arab Spring,"*
*Global Issues in Context Online Collection.*
*Detroit, MI: Gale, 2014.*

authorities responsible for organising the vote in a largely orderly manner'. Orderly is one way of describing the preemptive arrest of opposition activists.

As for the broadsheet supporters of the Arab Spring, and later the military coup, their position seems to have become a little more critical. So having praised the military for bringing down an elected government and, in the words of the *New*

York Times columnist David Brooks, pointing out that Morsi's election showed that the Egyptian people 'lack the mental equipment to govern', many pundits have changed their tune. The news that 'the military-backed government has shifted its attention to secular activists' and that 'the most genuine and committed supporters of a secular liberal order in Egypt [are now] sitting in Cairo's Tora prison' has led to a growing willingness to point out that Emperor al-Sisi is wearing dictator's clothes.

## Time to Face the Truth

But again, the double standards are still at work. It's striking that it is only since the Egyptian authorities started arresting the secular, liberal-ish activists Westerners approve of—the likes of Ahmed Maher [youth organizer and political activist], Mohammed Adel [youth organizer and political activist], Ahmed Douma [an activist and blogger] and Alaa Abdel Fattah [an activist and blogger]—that al-Sisi's regime has started to look like the authoritarian military dictatorship it always was. When it was massacring Muslim Brotherhood supporters, when it was rounding up and arresting supporters of Morsi, those currently up in arms about the crackdown on secular types could barely raise an eyebrow, let alone lift a pen in condemnation.

So, yes, what has happened in Egypt ought to chill us. It ought to command the attention of anyone who cares about defending freedom, even if—no, especially if—it's the freedom of those like the Muslim Brotherhood we might not like. Yet so superficial and so selective is the democratic commitment of Western pundits and politicians, so illiberal and freedom-doubting are their basic impulses, that what has happened in Egypt has barely been recognised for the oppressive military coup d'état that it is. It seems that democracy for these one-time champions of the Arab Spring has nothing to do with freedom, the chance for people to determine collectively their own future. Rather, it is seen as little more than a means to what Western leaders and media supporters hoped would be the right end. And if they don't like the end, if they don't like who the Egyptians vote for, then, just like a tap, their support for democracy can be turned off.

> "One of the longer-term trends U.S. policy makers should prepare for is a regional shift in power that will come about as a result of the Arab Spring, with Egypt emerging in a strengthened leadership position."

# Egypt Will Rise Again

*Ross Harrison*

*Ross Harrison is an author, political commentator, and instructor at Georgetown University and the University of Pittsburgh. In the following viewpoint, he predicts that Egypt will emerge as a stronger regional power, while Iran, Syria, Iraq, and Lebanon will fade in influence. Harrison contends that Egypt will be pushed to assume this enhanced regional role because of the weakened political structure in Syria and Iraq, and because it will focus on developing a robust foreign policy that addresses the challenges affecting the entire region. Egypt's strengthened regional role will be supported by the United States, which will view Egypt as a useful counterweight to Iran's political influence. Harrison asserts that it will be challenging for American leaders to focus on the long term and see past Egypt's current challenges to protect American and Egyptian interests.*

As you read, consider the following questions:

1. What former Egyptian president does the author identify as the figure who led the country's nationalist revival?

2. According to the viewpoint, in what year was Egyptian president Anwar Sadat assassinated?

3. What relationship does the author view as a striking example of how political weakness of Arab governments can be exploited by non-Arab powers?

While Washington struggles to keep pace with the crises that are currently engulfing individual Arab countries, it also needs to consider what might lie ahead for the Middle East region as a whole. Paradoxically, there is greater ability to foresee longer-term regional trends than there is in predicting shorter-term outcomes in individual countries. Policy makers, unable to forecast what type of government will surface next in Egypt, or when Syria's civil war might wind down, would get a clearer picture of the future by stepping back and paying attention to these longer-term regional trends.

One of the longer-term trends U.S. policy makers should prepare for is a regional shift in power that will come about as a result of the Arab Spring, with Egypt emerging in a strengthened leadership position. Along with this shift in power will likely be a corresponding reduction of regional power for Iran, and for the Arab countries in Iran's sphere of influence, namely Syria, Iraq and Lebanon.

How is the argument for a rising Egypt even plausible given its current political turmoil and economic torpor?

First of all, Egypt's internal politics is likely to push it towards a stronger regional role. Because the country is likely to be politically divided and economically hobbled for some time, it will be difficult for the next government to generate legitimacy by domestic means alone. A more robust Egyptian foreign policy, focused on the vexing issues facing the Arab world, is likely to be part of a strategy for creating regime legitimacy and domestic political stability. Second, Egypt will likely be pulled towards a stronger regional role by conditions of instability and weakened political structures in Syria and Iraq. So Egypt will be pushed into a regional role by its domestic politics, and pulled into that role by regional politics.

Let's examine how Egypt's domestic politics is likely to push it towards a strengthened role in the region. As politically divided as Egypt seems today, and as isolated from regional politics as the country was under former president Hosni Mubarak, Egyptians are fiercely nationalistic when it comes to both domestic and regional issues. There is historic evidence for this, particularly under former president Gamal Abdel Nasser, who led Egypt's nationalist revival and assumed a regional leadership role under the banner of Arab nationalism in the 1950s and 1960s.

Nasser overplayed his strategic hand, and tragically for Egypt and the broader Arab world, he fell victim to his own bravado. His Arab nationalist movement collapsed after the humiliating defeat by Israel in the 1967 war. While the Arab political movement was discredited by the defeat, Egyptian nationalism continued to drive Egypt towards regional involvement. Nasser's successor, Anwar Sadat, picked up the regional leadership mantle by planning and launching a surprise attack on Israel by Egyptian and Syrian forces in 1973.

After Sadat's assassination in 1981, his successor, Hosni Mubarak, shrunk Egypt's regional role, keeping the country insulated from Arab politics for the next thirty years. But what the Nasser and Sadat eras teach us is that Egypt's diminished role in the region under Mubarak was very much a historic anomaly, not the country's natural predisposition. Unlike his predecessors, the situation Mubarak found himself in militated against a robust regional role. He inherited from Sadat a country that was a virtual pariah because of its peace treaty with Israel, that had been expelled from the Arab League, and that was plagued with domestic and regional legitimacy problems. Moreover, having learned a lesson about the perils of a high-wire regional foreign policy from his predecessor's assassination, Mubarak's instincts were to avoid rocking the boat and tread softly on the regional and international stage.

Notwithstanding Egypt's long political hibernation under Mubarak, Egyptians today are no less nationalistic than before. The protests of 2011 that led to Mubarak's overthrow, and the street demonstrations of 2013 that led to the premature termination of President Morsi's reign, are prima facie evidence of this. But Egypt's history instructs us that nationalism has both an internal and external face. No Egyptian government can successfully play the nationalist card or generate legitimacy unless it solves the internal political and economic problems that are plaguing the country today. But Egypt's new leaders are likely to play to nationalism's external face in order to buy themselves time (and legitimacy) as they tackle the vexing economic problems the country faces. This means that regional foreign-policy issues, which have been somewhat dormant for many years, are likely to float back to the surface.

In addition to being pushed into a regional role by its domestic politics, Egypt will also be pulled into that role by instability and weakness in Syria, Iraq and Lebanon. There are several reasons for this. First of all, Egypt is likely to emerge from its crisis earlier and in better political shape than Syria and Iraq, whose legitimacy problems run deeper and pose a greater threat to the existence of the state itself. Second of all, the inherent weakness of these states and the potential for a redrawing of the borders imposed by the European colonial powers will create demand for regional leadership. A more politically viable Egypt would be positioned well to fill that role. Lastly, Egypt, as the largest Arab country, is the natural counterweight to Turkey and Iran, non-Arab states whose rising regional power could be perceived as threatening to more feeble

## The Accomplishments of Gamal Abdel Nasser

Gamal Abdel Nasser (1918–1970) was an Egyptian political leader and hero of much of the Arab world. His devotion to Arab unity and a strongly anti-imperialist ideology came to be called "Nasserism."

The accomplishments of the Nasser regime (agrarian reform, mobilization of the people, industrialization, vast social measures) were carried out despite both internal and external opposition. The leftist elements were integrated into the regime; the rightists were put under control. Abroad, support was obtained from the Soviet bloc of nations without breaking all ties with the West. The crisis of the third war with Israel, in June of 1967, reaffirmed Nasser's popular support and led to a certain amount of internal liberalization.

Nasser was a pragmatic politician, faithful above all to Egyptian patriotism. He disliked violence and extreme revolutionary activities. Although he was attracted for a time by the dream of political hegemony over the Arab world, his desires were nevertheless tempered by the needs and circumstances of the moment. His primary goal was always the development of Egypt into a modern nation with no sacrifice of complete independence. He died on September 28, 1970.

*"Gamal Abdel Nasser,"*
Encyclopedia of World Biography, *Biography in Context.*
*Detroit, MI: Gale, 1998.*

Arab governments. Moreover, Iran and Turkey have chosen different sides in the Syrian conflict, positioning Egypt to be more of a neutral broker. Should there be a redrawing of Syrian or Iraqi borders, or a political collapse in these countries,

Turkey and Iran are more likely than Egypt to be perceived as exploiting the political wreckage. Turkey's separate energy relationship with Iraqi Kurdistan, bypassing the Iraqi government in Baghdad, is a striking example of how political weakness of Arab governments can be exploited by non-Arab powers.

What would a strengthened regional role for Egypt mean for the United States? While Egypt in the future is likely to be less pliant than it was under Mubarak's leadership, the potential for it to serve as a counterweight to Iran's political influence in the region could serve U.S. interests. Even in the unlikely event that Egypt once again transitions to an Islamic-leaning government, the need to maintain support and legitimacy will mean its foreign policy will likely tack more in the direction of Arab issues, and less towards an Islamic agenda. Moreover, Iran's influence in the Arab world, and its success in playing a spoiler role through its proxies Hezbollah and Syria, was in large part due to a leadership vacuum in the Arab world. A restoration of Egyptian leadership could crowd out Iran's influence on Arab issues and make it more difficult for Iran to play the spoiler role on Arab-Israeli issues.

But the rise of Egypt could also pose a challenge to the United States. While Egypt is unlikely to pose a direct threat to U.S. regional interests, it is likely to be more independent in its views and actions than it ever was under former president Mubarak. This means that on some issues U.S. and Egyptian interests may converge, while on others they might be in direct conflict. Because of this, the United States will need to re-gear for a foreign policy less dependent on "hard-wired" Cold War–style alliances and focus more on creating issue-specific coalitions. Diplomatic and intelligence capabilities will need to reflect the need to work with a more independent Egypt, which won't reflexively follow the U.S. lead, but instead will need to be persuaded on a case-by-case basis of the merits of the U.S. position. But first the United States has to see beyond the current crises and pay attention to the longer-term trends of the Arab Spring, which involve shifts in the regional balance of power. Only the future will tell if Washington is up to that challenge.

> *"Three years on, as I consider what's left of the Egyptian revolution, I find that respect for its agenda lives on—but only for some."*

# Egypt's Democratic Revolution Has Stalled

## H.A. Hellyer

*H.A. Hellyer is a fellow at the Brookings Institution, a research associate at Harvard University, and an associate fellow of the Royal United Services Institute. In the following viewpoint, he maintains that the Egyptian revolution remains unfinished, waylaid by powerful political movements such as the Muslim Brotherhood and the counterrevolution that put the military junta in power. He views Egyptian society as divided by political strife, with one side supporting the Muslim Brotherhood, an Islamist political movement that stoked sectarianism, encouraged vigilantism, and eventually sparked a constitutional crisis; and the other side supporting the military junta, which has wasted no time in cracking down on political dissent and violating civil liberties and human rights when it grabbed power. Hellyer con-*

H.A. Hellyer, "Lessons from a Lost Revolution: Egypt's Fate Still Hangs in the Balance," *Salon*, February 11, 2014. Copyright © 2014 by Salon. This article first appeared in Salon.com, at www.Salon.com. An online version remains in the Salon archives. Reprinted with permission.

*tends that there are still those in Egypt fighting the good fight
and notes that these mavericks are attacked from both sides of
the political divide.*

As you read, consider the following questions:

1. According to the author, on what day was Egyptian
   president Mohamed Morsi ousted from power?

2. What two Egyptians does the author consider as examples of a more open and accepting wing of the Muslim Brotherhood?

3. What two Egyptian media outlets does Hellyer consider
   as ones that hold all sides of the conflict to account?

My life has been split between Europe and the Arab world,
but in the winter of 2010, I decided to move from one
home in England to another in Egypt. My family had grown
with the arrival of a baby, and I wanted a quieter, simpler life.
A few weeks later, I was in Tahrir Square, witnessing the birth
of a revolution. For three years, I watched that revolution, and
offered analysis of it as well for a number of news outlets. But
above all else, I was in deep solidarity with it.

Today, two major forces vie to speak in that revolution's
name—but they're interested in power, not in the ideals of
dignity and liberty. A rare few indeed are invested in the
revolution's demands for freedom and justice, and I continue
to marvel at the dignity on display, at the refusal to allow
their faith in a better Egypt to die.

Three years ago today [that is, February 11, 2011], the
night of [Hosni] Mubarak's resignation, I was in Tahrir Square,
hoping along with so many others that the revolution would
deliver a better future. Those were the days when revolutionaries, I among them, felt that anything was possible. As subsequent events unfolded to deflate that optimism—as the Supreme Council for the Armed Forces botched the opportunity

for a just transition—I shared in the revolutionaries' disappointment. When they marched courageously for justice, I marched alongside them, and asked for their courage. When they mourned their dead, my heart ached with them. When I was asked to analyze their cause, was I analyzing my own?

I watched as those revolutionaries split their votes between opposing presidential candidates the following year, saw many of them back Mohamed Morsi [a leading figure in the Muslim Brotherhood, an Islamic political group] over Mubarak's last prime minister in the final round of voting. Afterwards, I watched the rapid disintegration of Morsi's popularity. Having continued to hope for a more just democracy, I criticized the conduct of the Muslim Brotherhood during Morsi's tenure, and warned against the increasing likelihood of a military intervention once his failures began rapidly to accumulate. I empathized with those activists who defiantly declared, "Despair is betrayal."

The realization that Morsi's political movement was about nothing more than the seizure of power was infuriating, to myself as much as to the revolutionaries. Nonetheless, while I supported early presidential elections, I didn't back the widespread protests against Morsi on June 30, 2013. Fearful of an outbreak of deadly clashes, I breathed a sigh of relief when those protests ended without violent turmoil. But his ouster by the military on July 3 was not a celebratory moment. I worried about the consequences of a non-revolutionary force co-opting a popular movement to advance its own agenda. But even then, I couldn't have imagined the counter-revolutionary momentum that would soon take hold.

## A Reassessment

Three years on, as I consider what's left of the Egyptian revolution, I find that respect for its agenda lives on—but only for some. Many of those who've watched the events unfolding, both in Egypt and in the West, seem to misunderstand not only the revolution itself, but also the conflict between the minority who back the Brotherhood's claims to 'legitimacy' and a majority who seem to have settled for the military's 'stability'. The revolution's marginal mavericks, who resist side-picking in favor of a fealty to the principles of the January 25th movement, have seen themselves branded as traitors or as mistresses of the military, depending on the ideology of the accuser.

Those few holding fast to the promise of revolution now exist in a lonely minority, but they haven't given up on salvaging the revolution. Neither have I.

## The Myth of the "Good" Brotherhood

Not everyone agrees with the perspective I just shared—including a few of my academic and professional colleagues in London and Washington. For years, we had found common cause objecting to the demonization of Arabs and Muslims, taking to task those on the far right who provided the intellectual ammunition for xenophobic attitudes, policies, and even violence. We jointly critiqued the dangerously counterproductive, U.S.-led "War on Terror" narrative, and the UK's counter-radicalization "Prevent" strategy. We celebrated the departure of Hosni Mubarak, agreed the military should stay out of politics, and looked forward to a new republic.

Yet, while I saw a genuine movement of Muslims and Christians rally against an Islamist president, a few of my colleagues conflated the Brotherhood's parochial style of Islamism with Islam as a whole. Where I identified a Brotherhood leadership that was permissive of sectarianism and vigilantism, some identified Morsi supporters as simply "the Muslims." So perhaps it was their justifiable commitment to anti-Islamophobia that led them to overlook the failings of the Morsi government.

Brotherhood members are of course Muslim. But then again, *most* Egyptians are. Indeed, Brotherhood opponents in

Egypt, too, are mostly Muslim. Many of them will describe themselves as religious, and many support a public role for religion. Among the non-Islamist religious establishment—and even in some segments of the Islamist political spectrum—Egyptians are split between those who oppose the Brotherhood, those who oppose the army, and those who oppose both. Partisans of all stripes show willingness to use religion for political advantage. The notion that the only good Muslims—or even good Islamists—are Morsi supporters is an easily discredited one.

Some considered the Brotherhood as an Arab-Muslim version of the German Christian Democrats—a political force rooted in religion, but essentially accepting of the major principles of pluralism and democracy. There was perhaps such a vision within the Brotherhood, but it belonged to a reformist trend that might have been vocal internationally, yet weak within. Representatives of that trend, such as Kamal El-Helbawy and Abdel Moneim Aboul Fotouh, spent much time mediating perceptions of the Brotherhood for many in London, Washington, and elsewhere. However, that peripheral trend was completely sidelined many years ago in favor of more radical intellectual influences, which came to dominate the Brotherhood leadership. That leadership led the Brotherhood through the post-Mubarak years, carrying on after he was overthrown in an even more right-wing direction. This leadership proved to be less interested in social justice and freedom than in political power.

Attempting to defend the Brotherhood even as it dashed revolutionary hopes, a few of my Western colleagues may have been reacting to the characterization of the Islamist group as some sort of terrorist bogeyman. They would be right to question this mistaken use of the term; over the past decade, I've objected strenuously in policy and academic circles when the Brotherhood was described as akin to al-Qaeda. But this modern-day Brotherhood, far from advancing the cause of pluralistic democracy, aligned the group's interests with those of the military junta, stoked sectarianism, and took no issue with encouraging its members to indulge in vigilantism as they felt necessary. The Brotherhood resisted—nay, aborted—efforts to establish transitional justice, and showed shocking stubbornness throughout, at a time when Egypt needed them to be leaders.

For these Western associates of mine, the Brotherhood is the "good guy" in this story of two sides, advocates for "freedom," contra those urging "militarism." At the height of the post-9/11 [referring to the September 11, 2001, terrorist attacks on the United States] War on Terror, my colleagues and I have problematized such crude, binary thinking; employing that logic now goes against the spirit of every effort we made.

## Ruptures in the City Victorious

All over the world, and throughout history, politics has divided families. Egypt is no exception. Wives and husbands; brothers and sisters; parents and children. Some side with the bad, others with the really ugly—but few, it seems, find themselves aligned with an uncomplicated *good*. If, in London and Washington, I've disagreed with a few former confederates on Egypt, I've been repelled on another level entirely by many in Cairo, due to their uniquely distasteful viewpoints.

I've known those who claimed during Morsi's presidency that they were for the advancement of human rights, and then turned a blind eye to human rights violations after Morsi's removal from power. Some of these people still, without irony, claim to be "liberal." Many of them would have been dismayed at the killings of protesters under Mubarak or Morsi. But their fury was mute after the "most serious incident of mass unlawful killings" of Egyptian civilians in modern history, as state forces killed hundreds of people in the aftermath of sit-ins and protests against the current military-backed interim government. These people rightly mourn the many who

## Hosni Mubarak

Hosni Mubarak became president of the Arab Republic of Egypt following the assassination of President Anwar Sadat in 1981. He continued his predecessor's policy of peace with Israel, while managing to win back diplomatic relations with the Arab states that cut themselves off from Egypt after Sadat decided to recognize the Jewish state's right to exist. Although for the most part Mubarak remained steadfast in working for peace in the Middle East, he did join the United States–led coalition in the Persian Gulf War of 1991 and sent Egyptian troops to aid in the liberation of Kuwait. With the subsequent defeat of Iraq and its president, Saddam Hussein, Mubarak—as president of the most populous Arab nation—became in the minds of many analysts the most powerful leader in the Arab world. While he remained a close ally of the West with his efforts to suppress Islamic militants, Egyptian citizens increasingly began to call for change. In February of 2011, Mubarak resigned from the presidency after mass political protests and international pressure evaporated what little support remained for his faltering regime.

*"Hosni Mubarak,"*
*Biography in Context. Detroit, MI: Gale, 2013.*

have been killed by Islamist militants, yet they see little wrong in the many thousands detained under dubious justifications. They say little or nothing about the new restrictions against assembly and the press. Without evidence, they willfully accept the arguments of fringe American conservatives who would associate the Brotherhood with al-Qaeda. And it is rare indeed to see them criticize any excess by the state.

On the other side of this divide, there are those delivering apologia for the Brotherhood, arguing Morsi was at worst guilty of understandable mismanagement. In this parallel narrative, opposition against him was minimal, and were he to run in presidential elections, he might even win. I've tried myself to directly discuss the collapse in public support to such Brotherhood supporters many times—drawing on my own work with the Gallup organization and other surveys—without much success.

They'll argue that if the Brotherhood lost any support, it was simply due to misinformation in the media—not because of transparent power grabs such as the extrajudicial decree in November 2012 intended to stymy the judiciary and push through the Brotherhood's constitution. It certainly wasn't because of gross mismanagement of Egypt's economy. Nor because Morsi and the Brotherhood publicly courted radicals that incited violence—which intensified after his ouster—or encouraged vigilantism to protect their institutions. No, it's just a conspiracy, and no progress is ever going to be appropriate, unless it is a reversal of the past eight months.

Just as proponents of the military unfairly conflate the Brotherhood with the radical militant cadres of the "Ansar Bayt al-Maqdis" group, Brotherhood figures deny even the existence of such militants, directly insinuating that any attacks by such are false flag operations, coordinated by the state. The threat of militant violence, however, is real—and other groups, sharing a nihilism based on their own form of dehumanization, are emerging. Their attacks have only increased in intensity and fury, spreading beyond the Sinai Peninsula into urban centers. It seems it is only a matter of time before they target civilians as well, and it is entirely possible such groups will draw more recruits from disaffected Brotherhood supporters in the future.

## Egypt's Last Mavericks

"If you are neutral in situations of injustice, you have chosen the side of the oppressor. If an elephant has its foot on the tail of a mouse and you say that you are neutral, the mouse will not appreciate your neutrality." Archbishop Desmond Tutu never spoke truer words. He spoke in reference to those who equivocated about apartheid, and chose "neutrality" instead of clear opposition to the oppressive South African regime. Against the current backdrop of violent polarization in Egypt—where not just the military rulers, but also their chief adversaries, are guilty of striking malfeasance—is there any good alternative?

My father, a veteran of the anti-apartheid movement in the UK, once described the apartheid regime as self-evidently evil, and the oppositional African National Congress as a sufficiently moral force with which to stand against that evil. There is no comparable political movement to stand behind in Egypt. But the intellectual heart of the revolution that began in Tahrir Square was always "speaking truth to power," regardless who held it. Doing so means rejecting the binary presumption of "picking sides," and instead holding both the military-backed regime and the Brotherhood accountable for their misdeeds.

There are those who remain true to that original revolutionary impulse, who reject the false choice of these two non-revolutionary forces. These mavericks, who focus on holding all to account, are not themselves above reproach. Indeed, they can and should be criticized for their own failings, missed opportunities, and strategic mistakes. But at every point, they've doggedly remained true to that core principle. In the process, they've lost some of their own to the violence in the streets. Others sit in jails, detained under the pretext of the new anti-protest law. But the scores of journalists, civil rights activists and human rights defenders that make up the core of this fledging movement have made a defiant choice.

It is they who continue the fight to call all to account, through certain media outlets like *Mada Masr* and *Daily News Egypt*—through rights organizations like the Egyptian Initiative for Personal Rights, the Cairo Institute for Human Rights Studies, and the Egypt office of Human Rights Watch.

I've been in Egypt for most of the mass killings over the past three years—and there have been more than a dozen, with fatalities reaching into the thousands. It is these mavericks that seek accountability for those deaths, regardless of the identity and political alignment of perpetrator and victim. It is they who try to find a space to voice themselves in new coalitions, like the "Way of the Revolution [Front]," and civil society organizations like the film collective "Mosireen." It was from these margins, these mavericks, that the revolution was born—and it is with them that it remains sustained.

When these revolutionaries reject the two major forces in Egypt, it comes at a price, and they have invited attacks from both. The state considers them dissenters, at a time where dissent seems akin to treason. An Egyptian version of McCarthyism [the practice of making accusations of disloyalty, subversion, or treason without proper evidence] infests much public discourse, as does a kind of neo-fascistic militarism; police brutality has claimed the lives of hundreds. Egypt's mavericks are exasperated by the idea that the growing insurgency means giving the interim government, its military backers, and state institutions a wide berth. There will always be an excuse to avoid holding the state to account. But account they must.

There is also no love lost between these mavericks and the Muslim Brotherhood leadership, which suspects, by some opaque logic, the unaligned revolutionaries are secretly pro-military. ("How would the Brotherhood have reacted," the fervently anti-military mavericks sarcastically retort, "had the military removed a president the Brotherhood had *opposed*?")

Talk of the security state returning is inappropriate—for it never truly left—but was the Brotherhood ever *really* interested in reforming that security apparatus? Or did it, as human rights activists would testify, instead try to co-opt that system, and use it to its own advantage? Critics remain convinced that what seduced the Brotherhood was not pragmatism or naïveté, but power, above any other concern.

## The Best Chance for Egypt

Caught amidst a dangerous game of zero-sum brinkmanship, it is ordinary Egyptians who truly suffer the most. While supporters of the two major political powers wish to claim moral clarity, neither group is likely to deliver on the demands of the revolution. Even as that revolution fades further away into memory, it remains to be Egypt's best chance at progress.

Activists in support of the January 25 revolution aren't angels: They've made mistakes from very early on. The revolution demanded more of them. Over the past three years, their idealism has become more battle-hardened. While they've not become Machiavellian operators, they've matured from their marginal roots. Yet they have to evolve even further.

These activists persist, and they will be the ones who continue to remind those of influence, and those in power, of one simple truth: The people of Egypt descended on Tahrir Square in 2011 to fight for dignity. They've made that choice to endure, to keep fighting for an alternative, to continue speaking truth to power.

They're not just the famous activists lavished with attention. They're the legions of pro-revolution Egyptians who are not known to the press, but who are even still fighting battle after battle in their own arenas, obscured to the non-Arabic-speaking international media. They exist nonetheless.

There would have been no Tahrir Square without these people, who formed the bedrock of an uprising that inspired the world. They haven't given up yet. While they continue what efforts they can, the story of the revolution of the 25th of January, 2011, still remains a story unfinished. As I traverse and try to understand their story, I recognise the truth of whether or not I've ever been an observer in their story—or a part of it.

> *"The revolution's ambition was to re-*
> *build the country using the capabilities*
> *of its people, who showed their bril-*
> *liant presence after a long and forced*
> *absence."*

# Egypt Is Hobbled by a Culture of Corruption and Cronyism

## Talal Salman

*Talal Salman is a journalist and founder of* As-Safir, *a daily Lebanese newspaper. In the following viewpoint, he offers his perspective as a Lebanese citizen on the challenges faced by Egypt's new government. Salman praises the brave leadership of General Abdel Fattah al-Sisi and the military regime that ousted former president Mohamed Morsi and circumvented the Muslim Brotherhood's power grab. He wonders, however, whether Sisi has the capability to act effectively as a civilian leader to meet the challenge of moving Egyptian society forward. As a leader, Sisi would have to address one of Egypt's biggest problems: wide-spread corruption and cronyism. Salman argues that because of this pervasive problem, which flourished under decades of military dictatorship in the twentieth century, Egypt is struggling.*

As you read, consider the following questions:

1. According to the author, how long did the last military rule last in Egypt, starting from the July 1952 revolution?

2. When was military rule established in Libya, according to Salman?

3. What severe test does the author identify that General Abdel Fattah al-Sisi will face when it comes to other Arab countries?

Does an Arab citizen outside of Egypt have the right to express an opinion regarding an "internal" Egyptian matter? Especially noting that the dramatic developments brought about by the communications revolution have erased borders, eliminated distance and turned the world into a big "village" with no secrets or the ability to limit repercussions on the pretext of sovereignty, or to prevent interference in a country's internal affairs?

Any Arab citizen in any of the countries of this great *umma* [nation] is interested in Egypt's presidential election and Egypt's developments of the past three years because they will affect his country, whether in the East or West, and because Egypt—when it is strong, as most Arabs wish it to be, or weak and abandons its responsibilities and resorts to isolation or to repudiating its Arab identity—occupies a post of leadership and reference for Arabs. And what Egypt decides affects the rest of the Arabs, whether negatively or positively.

## One Opinion on Egypt and Its Future

Regarding my opinion on the presidential elections in Egypt, especially after field marshal Abdel Fattah al-Sisi resigned from his position as commander in chief of the armed forces and decided to run in the presidential election, here are some observations.

There is a big difference between the objectives of the glorious and unprecedented revolution and the political result, namely the arrival of the military to the presidency once again. The revolution's ambition was to rebuild the country using the capabilities of its people, who showed their brilliant presence after a long and forced absence.

The issue is not about Sisi personally, who managed—via a brave decision and in a defining moment in modern Egyptian history—to provide the anti–Muslim Brotherhood popular movement with the ability to oust the "regime" that the Brotherhood tried to establish by circumventing and duping the revolution, whose prominent slogan was, "Down, down with military rule." The issue is about the irony that the revolution that called for the fall of military rule now finds itself facing a single presidential candidate that headed the military establishment, and that this candidate is seen as the "savior" from the rule of the Brotherhood.

## A Key Question

Will the soldier who took the courageous decision to lead the popular movement to overthrow the rule of the Brotherhood (which was expecting to stay in power indefinitely) be able to present himself to the Egyptians (and later to the Arabs and to the world) as a civilian president who is qualified and capable of renewing Egypt's political life using the living forces that sparked two massive revolutions in less than three years?

Military rule in Egypt lasted 60 years, from the July 23, 1952, revolution until the beginning of July 2013, with an interlude of no more than a year under the rule of the Muslim Brotherhood. That group provoked the Egyptians and pushed them to the streets to bring down Brotherhood rule. To achieve that, the Egyptians chose to put aside for a while the "Down, down with military rule" slogan, and they took to the streets by the millions. Will those respond to today's call by the [former] commander in chief of the armed forces Gen. Sisi?

So the matter is simply this: A military man is about to take over the presidency and general command of state affairs in the largest Arab country, which had been expected to make history after the bitter experiences of military rule in many Arab countries.

## Military Rule in the Arab Region

The first coup attempt in the region was in Iraq under the monarchy of the British mandate in the 1940s. The rule in the Syrian republic has been continuously under military rule from the spring of 1949 (directly after the defeat in Palestine) until today, in one form or another.

Military rule in Egypt started with the revolution in July 1952 and lasted until the [Tahrir] Square uprising at the start of 2012. In Iraq, military rule began on July 14, 1958. In Yemen, military rule started with the outbreak of the great popular revolution and the evacuation of French colonization in 1965. In Libya, it started on Sept. 1, 1969. In Sudan, the military has governed for the past 40 years, with limited interludes of civilian rule. In Tunisia, the military deposed Habib Bourguiba, then Zine El Abidine Ben Ali ruled for three decades. In Algeria, civilian rule for the revolution only lasted for three years, then the military took over . . . [and is still in place] today.

This means that the military has dominated power in the largest and most important Arab states, from east to west, over the past 60 years. So military rule can be considered responsible for the changes and disturbances, the progress and setbacks experienced by those countries, with a disastrous final outcome, as evidenced by the conditions of those countries after more than 60 years of "achievements" by military regimes.

## Corruption and Cronyism

Perhaps the most dangerous of these "achievements" is that the popular movement, in its parties and its political, trade, professional, elite and cultural organizations, has almost disappeared because of the repression and the buying of loyalty, position and privilege. Arab countries have almost become barren deserts, with no talent nor competencies to offer, because the choice before talented citizens was the following: If you show loyalty to the sultan you will be praised, and if you oppose him you will be marginalized and forced to leave the country and sell your talents to foreigners. If you decide to be confrontational and challenge the rule, you will be jailed.

It is no accident that ancient nations such as Egypt, Iraq and Syria are crumbling and falling behind in all kinds of production or that their excellent talent has left, and that corruption prevails throughout the government as a result of corrupt rule, tyranny and a prevailing military logic that says "obey, then object." Algeria, Libya and Yemen can be added to this list.

The elites have emigrated to where they can profit from their talents and live a life without suppression. Many have chosen to live under the harsh conditions of the "comfortable exile." Countries lost the citizens with the best abilities to build them. Meanwhile, military cliques have taken over leadership positions and opened the door for opportunists, hypocrites and incompetents. Corruption has spread through the government, bribery has become common and rulers have surrounded themselves with corrupt people and isolated themselves from the people's concerns and their legitimate right to progress.

Certainly, Egypt and its prominent government are now more backward than in the 1960s, regardless of claims. Education has gotten immeasurably worse, the government is more corrupt, countryside inhabitants have moved into the cities and government services are fueled by bribery.

## The Regional Challenge

That's regarding the interior. On the Arab level, Egypt's next president will be facing a severe test: The regimes that can help him are not free. They must refer to the "decision-makers," who are major faraway states that can be summed up as the United States of America, its interests, positions and ties, and one strategic ally in the region: Israel.

Becoming president is a first step on a risky road. This heavy task cannot be performed by an individual, a group of individuals, a party or group of parties. Egypt is facing a challenge: to restore itself, its spirit, its role and its capacity to deliver. Sisi has shown the extraordinary courage to take on that great mission.

I hope that Egypt regains its health and its role in making a better future for its people and for the *umma*, which has honored Egypt by putting it in the leadership position.

> "The failure to achieve all of one's political goals is the price of democratic politics. The refusal to accept this price may lead to the kind of political disaster we are now witnessing in Egypt."

# Egypt's Military Coup Could Doom Democracy

*Mohammad Fadel*

*Mohammad Fadel is a writer, political analyst, and a professor at the University of Toronto. In the following viewpoint, he analyzes the failure of the democratic transition in Egypt. Fadel maintains that the revolutionaries did not have a sufficient appreciation of the challenges they would face and were too ideologically rigid to compromise or to realize that the outcome of the democratic process often conflicts with one's political ideals and goals. Instead of compromising and trying to work within the existing system, the revolutionaries opened the door for military intervention and backed a coup against the democratically elected administration of Mohamed Morsi. This decision, he contends, may have doomed democracy in Egypt. He posits that Egypt will not have a stable democracy if it does not overcome its legacy of mismanagement, corruption, and weak democratic institutions.*

As you read, consider the following questions:

1. According to Fadel, what candidate withdrew from the presidential elections of 2012?

2. What action did Egyptian president Mohamed Morsi take in November 2012 that is considered to be the final blow to his administration, according to the author?

3. What Egyptian politician does the author identify as barred from running for president in 2012 until the courts rescinded the ban?

On February 11, 2011, after eighteen days of protests, Hosni Mubarak resigned as president of Egypt. Now, three years later, the Egyptian security state appears to have reestablished political control of the country.

Why did the democratic transition fail? Answers range widely. Some blame the poorly designed transition process, which made trust among different political groups unachievable. Others point to a lack of leadership within Egypt's political organizations, particularly the Muslim Brotherhood. Still others focus on a devastating economic crisis that post-Mubarak governments could never address given the political divisions within the country.

These explanations are plausible and not mutually exclusive. But they all miss something important. The January 25 revolution was also a striking failure of political theory. More precisely, it was a failure of the theories embraced by the most idealistic revolutionaries. Their demands were too pure; they refused to accord any legitimacy to a flawed transition—and what transition is not flawed?—that could only yield a flawed democracy. They made strategic mistakes because they did not pay enough attention to Egypt's institutional, economic, political, and social circumstances. These idealists generally were politically liberal. But the problem does not lie in liberalism itself. The problem lies in a faulty understanding of the implications of political liberalism in the Egyptian context—an insufficient appreciation of factors that limited what could reasonably be achieved in the short term. A more sophisticated liberalism would have accounted for these realities.

## The Balance of Forces

Although the masses in Tahrir Square appeared unified on the day Mubarak fell, three broad groups were vying for power.

The first, associated with the military, took a *minimalist* view: The revolution was simply about removing Mubarak and his cronies from power, and ensuring that his son, Gamal Mubarak, did not succeed him to the presidency. Given this group's desire to preserve as much as possible of Mubarak's order (without Mubarak), it was able to reconcile with old-regime elements. This first group originally lacked a distinctive ideology, but it eventually adopted a nationalist, sometimes even xenophobic, posture that distinguished it from the cosmopolitanism of Islamist, liberal, and socialist revolutionaries.

According to a second group, the revolution aimed at broad reforms of the Egyptian state without uprooting it entirely. For this *reformist* group, the crisis stemmed from corruption. Mubarak, they argued, had undermined the state's integrity by usurping its institutions to fulfill his and his allies' personal and political ends. The revolution needed to reform the state's institutions so that they would meet the formal requirements of a legal order, accountable to the public will. Formal democracy was a crucial demand of this group because it was seen as the only way to ensure that the state would not again be hijacked to further the interests of a narrow group of Egyptian elites. The Muslim Brotherhood and its allies belonged to this second group.

The third group, composed largely of young Egyptians, understood the revolution as an attempt to fundamentally restructure state and society. The revolution provided an opportunity to create a virtuous state. Doing so would, however, require a complete rupture with the ancien régime. This *radical* group had an ambivalent relationship with formal democracy. Although elections were desirable, the most important goal was the substantive transformation of the state and society. "Revolutionary legitimacy" trumped whatever legitimacy formal representative democracy could provide.

The support enjoyed by each of these three groups remains uncertain. No one disputes that the youth, the third group, served as the revolutionary vanguard, having planned and executed the anti-regime demonstrations on January 25. The Muslim Brotherhood joined later, and the military, for obvious reasons, was the last to take up the banner.

## The Role of the Military

Still, one should not exclude the military from the revolutionary coalition. The protesters at Tahrir welcomed the military, which they believed to be more sympathetic to their cause than the detested police. Demonstrators treated the military as a legitimate authority. For example, when protesters caught agents provocateurs working for the regime, they were turned over to the military.

Other actions also underscored the willingness of Tahrir revolutionaries to recognize the continued legitimacy of at least parts of the old order. For example, prominent liberal lawyers within the revolutionary camp continued to abide by the constitution that Mubarak had put in place in the waning years of his presidency. This constitution included a series of amendments, adopted in spite of gross procedural irregularities, which were intended to ensure his son's succession. During the revolution, one liberal lawyer even published an appeal to Mubarak in the *Washington Post* demanding that he perform the formal steps required of a legal transition.

The more restrained interpretations of the revolution continued to have strong support among Egyptians even when

Mubarak resigned. Subsequent elections confirmed this. In the March 19th referendum, voters favored a quick transition and rejected radicals' appeals to complete a draft constitution before selecting a new government. In the subsequent parliamentary elections, Islamist-affiliated parties won almost 70 percent of the seats, while post-revolutionary liberal parties took only 10 percent. And in the presidential elections of 2012, with Mohamed ElBaradei withdrawn from the race, the liberals could not even field a candidate. The top two vote-getters in the first round, Ahmed Shafiq, Mubarak's last prime minister, and Mohamed Morsi, of the Muslim Brotherhood, were affiliated, respectively, with the minimalist and reformist camps.

Whatever else can be said about the political preferences of Egyptians as revealed by their post-revolutionary voting patterns, elections demonstrated that a successful and peaceful democratic transition would require a coalition of minimalists, reformists, and radicals. Each group would have to accommodate the other two.

## The Challenge of Pluralism

Accommodations are hardly unusual in societies emerging from a long period of authoritarian rule. Consider Chile, where General [Augusto] Pinochet was granted immunity in the aftermath of his bloody regime. All over Latin America, citizens accepted a substantial continuing role for free market economics, even though it had been a tool of dictators. Successful democratic transition inevitably requires some degree of compromise with old ways.

The challenge Egyptians faced throughout the transition was to build an inclusive polity in the face of their deep divisions. They could resolve these divisions either by suppressing disagreements through a forceful exercise of state power or by competing at the ballot box. The former strategy requires massive state violence in the short term and almost always

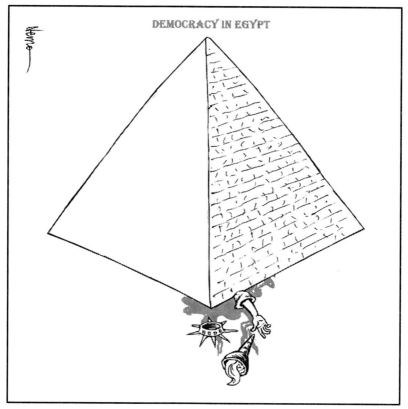

© Nemo/Cartoonstock.com.

leads to suspension of formal democracy, without any guarantee of a return to democracy in the medium or long term. The latter strategy involves less force, establishes at least the formal elements of democratic rule, and preserves the possibility of additional democratic gains in the future, even if it requires concessions to undemocratic or illiberal political groups in the present and is marked occasionally by episodes of political violence.

Both liberal and Islamic political theories endorse the second option. Traditional Islamic political theory prioritizes social peace in circumstances where achieving a more ideal polity would require widespread violence. Preserving social peace is also a crucial moral value of such political thinkers as

Thomas Hobbes and John Rawls. These theories applied in Egypt: a formally democratic regime that allowed for fair and nonviolent competition over political office was the only means of including all three of Egypt's political forces and thus the most likely to preserve social peace. Any attempt to suppress one of the three groups, on the other hand, would contradict this fundamental moral precept and would launch the country into civil war or else result in the imposition of emergency law. Both outcomes would foreclose meaningful politics.

From a Rawlsian perspective, Egypt's divisions meant that social peace could only be achieved through a constitution establishing a temporary agreement among the parties. Such a constitution could do no more than guarantee formally democratic procedures of governance. It could not satisfy the requirements of justice, since it would be grounded in a particular balance of social power rather than an overlapping consensus on a conception of justice. Nevertheless, such a constitution, in Rawls's view, is usually a necessary step toward the establishment of a just, well-ordered society.

## Another Paradigm

The 14th-century Arab Muslim political thinker Ibn Khaldūn's tripartite typology of regimes—natural, rational, and Islamic—is consistent, in broad terms, with Rawls's analysis. Natural states are based on relations of domination between the ruler and the ruled, restrained only by the limitations of the ruler's actual power. Rational and Islamic states, by contrast, impose moral restraints on the exercise of political power. According to Ibn Khaldūn, rational and Islamic regimes transcend the relations of domination characteristic of natural regimes and establish overlapping conceptions of the common *secular* good. Ibn Khaldūn's rational and Islamic regimes both can foster the convergence in political morality that—like Rawls's overlapping consensus—characterizes a just constitution. Critically, this convergence or consensus must occur organically. Ibn Khaldūn argued that coerced adherence to Islamic law fails to produce virtuous subjects. Likewise, coerced imposition of even a just constitution cannot produce an effective system of justice if large numbers of citizens are incapable of freely adhering to its terms.

Although procedural democracy by itself did not promise the radicals the substantive changes they hoped for in the short term, it did offer the possibility of social peace and an opportunity to generate, over time, a broader consensus on the fundamental questions of how to establish a just and effective state worthy of citizens' freely given allegiance. It also offered the foundation of a more liberal political order.

## Morsi's Constitutional Declaration

The most powerful post-revolutionary political actors in Egypt accepted a pragmatic option: They rejected radicalism and endorsed procedural democracy. When Morsi moved in November 2012 to insulate his decisions and the content of the 2012 constitution from judicial review, he was following the pragmatic course. Proponents of a liberal constitution objected, but their aims were not achievable without strife.

Most commentary points to Morsi's November 2012 declaration as the final blow to the Muslim Brotherhood's relationship with the liberal and radical revolutionaries, effectively setting in motion the events that led to the July 2013 coup.

Morsi was hardly the first Egyptian politician to issue such a decree. The military had used constitutional declarations regularly throughout the transition process in order to ensure that a formal legal order would remain in place. Morsi's goal was not outlandish either. He intended to prevent the judiciary from interfering with the constitutional drafting process so that a text could be completed in accordance with the provisions of the transitional road map, which had been approved by the March 2011 referendum. The radicals interpreted Morsi's decree as an intolerable assault on democracy, which confirmed their suspicions that Morsi and the Muslim Brotherhood were attempting to create a new kind of authoritarian state.

## The Role of Religion

The real issue, however, was the makeup of the Constituent Assembly and the substance of the constitution it would draft. The parties arrived at a deal, including the semi-presidential structure of the state—with executive power shared by a prime minister and popularly elected president—but the role of religion was a sticking point. Because Parliament had selected the members of the Constituent Assembly, and because Islamists had won Parliament, Islamists dominated the Constituent Assembly. Liberals argued, not unreasonably, that those parliamentary elections exaggerated Islamists' long-term political strength. Liberals also thought that the draft sacrificed or limited too many personal rights and freedoms in the name of religion, morality, and family values. They argued that the constitution would not be legitimate unless it was a consensual document capable of gaining acceptance by all significant social groups in Egypt.

The individual rights provisions of the constitution were clearly deficient from the perspective of international human rights law. In particular, the attempt to limit personal rights in the name of respect for traditional religious values does not comport with wider commitments to liberty. Liberal dissidents, however, never faced up to the reality that Egypt is divided on these personal rights. Should the state underwrite freedom of expression even if that enables blasphemy and apostasy? Should gender equality override religious rules, Christian or Muslim, particularly in the context of family law? Given that so many Egyptians disagree with the liberal position on these matters, it is hard to understand what the demand for a consensual constitution recognizing personal rights could have meant in practical terms.

The argument that the Constituent Assembly unreasonably exaggerated the strength of Islamist parties was plausible, but even granting this point, any democratic process would have placed a significant bloc of Islamists in the Constituent Assembly. So there was no democratic path for liberals to establish a constitution that secured the personal rights and freedoms they sought.

## A Growing Divide

By the time Morsi issued his November 2012 declaration, constitutional deliberations had effectively ground to a halt. From Morsi's perspective, the declaration was the only means available to prevent the Supreme Constitutional Court from dissolving the Constituent Assembly. He had reasonable grounds to worry that the court was prepared to intervene. A case demanding dissolution was pending, and the court had already issued two rulings that interfered in the democratic transition: one disbanding Egypt's first freely elected Parliament since 1952, the second overturning a law that attempted to bar old-regime elements, such as Shafiq from running for the presidency. The dissidents' boycott of the Constituent Assembly's deliberations was a not-so-subtle sign to the court that, as far as they were concerned, its intervention would be welcome. In light of the court's opposition and the fast-approaching deadline for completion of the draft constitution, Morsi felt he had no choice but to cut the court out.

There is little doubt that Morsi, as the democratically elected president, was the more legitimate arbiter of this dispute. The court is not democratically accountable, and the draft constitution could not come into effect unless it won approval in a popular referendum. While one might disagree with Morsi's methods, it is reasonable to conclude that he acted in accordance with his responsibilities as the only democratically accountable official in the country.

## The New Constitution

To describe his actions as a naked power grab, as ElBaradei suggested at the time, requires a presumption of bad faith inconsistent with democratic commitments. The radicals' violent opposition to the November declaration would only have been justified if the constitution Morsi acted to protect failed to promote a pluralistic and inclusive *political* system. This was not the case. The 2012 constitution provided a more open political system than had prevailed prior to the revolution. It increased formal political rights, reduced the power of the president, and increased the power of the prime minister and the Parliament.

These changes were meaningful. For the first time, anyone could form a political party or publish in print without the prospect of government censorship. By contrast, during the Mubarak era, the formation of political parties required the state's approval, thereby ensuring that no party capable of challenging the ruling National Democratic Party could develop. Under the new constitution, the president would be limited to serving two terms, would face stricter rules on declaring states of emergency, and would no longer be able to dismiss the prime minister. Parliament was newly empowered to withdraw confidence from the government. And the president would be required to select the prime minister from the largest party in Parliament.

The new constitution also boosted the capacity of the political branches by leaving open the content of many rights. Limitations on personal rights could only become operational upon the passage of positive law. The same was true of the provision contemplating military trials for civilians: Egypt's future governments had the power to reduce the jurisdiction of military courts or to eliminate it through legislation. And though the constitution did not recognize a universal right to religious exercise—protection is limited to followers of the three Abrahamic religions—it did not prevent the state from doing so in the future by statute.

This structure reduced the influence of the courts—in particular the Supreme Constitutional Court—by vesting the power to define rights in the political branches. This was a reasonable constitutional strategy in a society characterized by sharp division on fundamental personal rights.

Indeed, from a Rawlsian perspective, we would expect such a society to adopt a constitution that guarantees only those political rights necessary for democratic participation in lawmaking. The 2012 constitution appeared to accomplish that, leaving the more contentious issues of individual rights to future deliberation. Unlike constitutions of nearby states, such as Morocco, the 2012 constitution did not entrench any provisions, including those on the role of Islam, as supra-constitutional norms impervious to amendment. Nor did it place any substantive, ideological limitations on the formation of secular political parties, provided that they were not organized on a discriminatory basis. It did not impose religious piety or a theological test as condition for public office. This ensured that the constitution would not privilege the Muslim Brotherhood, other Islamist parties, or even the role of Islam itself above other provisions of the constitution.

## Democratic Faith

Even in a well-ordered, just society, Rawls argued, a polity may in some cases legitimately restrict the liberty of con-science of the intolerant, but only when there is a "reasonable expectation that not doing so will damage the public order which the government should maintain." While Egypt is not a well-ordered society in Rawls's sense, his principle casts light on how liberals should have reacted to the prospect of a military-led coup against an illiberal elected president and his illiberal political party. Extrapolating from Rawls's treatment of restrictions on liberty of conscience, we might say that preservation of the constitutional order is the only justification for such an intervention, and this claim is only legitimate when it is based on objective evidence, widely accessible, demonstrating that the threat to the lawful public order is not "merely possible or in certain cases even probable, but reasonably certain or imminent."

It is hard to judge that Morsi's conduct as president, however disappointing, crossed this threshold. Many radical revolutionaries justified their support for Morsi's removal not on the grounds that his actions represented an imminent threat to the political order, but rather on the grounds that Morsi did not confront the military and the police with sufficient vigor. In their eyes, he thus betrayed the revolution.

It is not clear, however, that Morsi had the power to transform these instruments of oppression in the year he was in office. The security forces were largely immune to Morsi's influence. They refused to protect the offices of the Muslim Brotherhood and its political party, the Freedom and Justice Party. Even businesses affiliated, or thought to be affiliated, with the Muslim Brotherhood could not rely on police or military protection. When the presidential palace was attacked during demonstrations in the wake of Morsi's constitutional decree, the security services were nowhere to be found. For Morsi's opponents, however, his failure to reform the security services was taken not as a sign of his weakness but as evidence that he and the Muslim Brotherhood were conspiring with the military and police to destroy the liberal and radical opposition.

## Three Strategies

Even less plausible than fears of a secret alliance between the Muslim Brotherhood and the security services was Egyptian liberals' belief that, in acting against Morsi, the military would promote democracy rather than restore the security state. Even if liberals were right about Morsi's and the Muslim Brotherhood's intentions, the only rational *democratic* strategy would have been to insist on parliamentary elections. There were at least three routes. If the opposition was able to win a two-thirds majority in upcoming parliamentary elections—which should have been easy if its claims about the universal unpopularity of the Muslim Brotherhood were true—it could have impeached Morsi. If found guilty at trial, he would have been removed from office. Even if unsuccessful in removing Morsi, such a strategy would have strengthened the cause of Egyptian democracy. A less dramatic step would have been to use Parliament's powers to withdraw confidence and appoint a new government. The other lawful option would have been to defeat Morsi or another Muslim Brotherhood candidate in the 2016 presidential elections.

Instead the opposition, including radical revolutionaries, demanded early presidential elections. But there were no legal grounds for hastening the election schedule. Morsi could only be ousted by military intervention, a strategy that discredited political parties as the representatives of the Egyptian people in favor of the military, police, and other state institutions. Thus did Egypt's most ardent democrats, under the banner of "the Revolution continues," forego constitutional options in favor of methods that would only advance authoritarianism.

The idealists who halted the democratic experiment failed to understand what democratic theorists have long recognized: that the very conditions that produce democracy—liberty and equality—also produce factionalism, instability, and violence. If clashes are not mediated through some acceptable institutional arrangement, they are likely to be resolved through despotism. This risk was especially palpable in Egypt given the dominant role that the military and security services have played since 1952.

## The Necessity of Compromise

Citizens in a democracy must accept compromise with political adversaries, which means that ideologues of every stripe will be disappointed. (Indeed, strident Islamists criticized

Morsi and the Muslim Brotherhood for making too many compromises with secular democrats.) The failure to achieve all of one's political goals is the price of democratic politics. The refusal to accept this price may lead to the kind of political disaster we are now witnessing in Egypt. Democracy, though grounded in the values of equality and liberty, is never born in societies perfectly reflecting these values. If they are realized, it is through the patient practice of democratic politics, even when its substantive outcomes conflict with one's political ideals. A successful democracy emerges gradually, inspired by the fierce, even fanatical, belief in the ability of democracy to improve the people's political virtue over time. Ironically Egypt's most radical democrats did not have this faith.

Liberal and radical critics of the Muslim Brotherhood failed to realize that the real choice in Egypt was not between an Islamic state and a civil state, but between a state based on some conception of the public good—religious or nonreligious—and one based on pure domination. In line with Ibn Khaldūn's argument about the relationship between the religious conception of the state and the rational one, there should have been plenty of scope for agreement between religious and secular democratic forces. Tragically, liberals underestimated the people's desire for security and their willingness to submit even to arbitrary and predatory power in order to achieve it. Their extra-legal strategies—protests, boycotts, and, finally, military intervention—gravely undermined the prospects that the emerging government would provide this crucial public good, opening the door for the return of the security state.

Egypt remains burdened by years of mismanagement and ill-considered policies that have been destructive of the common good, promoted corruption, and enfeebled the state's non-security functions. Egypt cannot have a stable democracy if it does not overcome this legacy. Only a government with democratic legitimacy can undertake the inevitably painful reforms. Repression of the Muslim Brotherhood—the country's most organized political group and one that, at least in principle, supports democratic practices—only puts off the day when Egypt can begin these needed reforms. By advocating military intervention in politics and, in too many cases, backing a coup against the legitimate government, the liberal and radical opposition have for the time being ruined the conditions for democracy. If the military-installed regime fails to establish political stability, which is a real possibility, Egypt faces the prospect of political chaos and even state failure.

This is the price of dogmatism in politics.

# Periodical and Internet Sources Bibliography

*The following articles have been selected to supplement the diverse views presented in this chapter.*

| | |
|---|---|
| *Australian* | "A New Tyranny Lurks in Egypt," April 2, 2014. |
| Benny Avni | "Arab Spring in Tatters," *Newsweek*, January 30, 2014. |
| Reuel Marc Gerecht | "The Great Collision: Egypt's Descent into Chaos," *Weekly Standard*, August 5, 2013. |
| Marie-Louise Gumuchian and Laura Smith-Spark | "Arab Spring Three Years On: Unsettled Waters or a Turning Tide?," Assyrian International News Agency, March 15, 2014. |
| Ian Lee and Heba Fahmy | "Is Egypt in the Midst of a Sexual Harassment Epidemic?," CNN, April 10, 2014. |
| John Lyons | "Egypt's Military Has Hijacked Experiment with Democracy," *Australian*, March 29, 2014. |
| Dan Murphy | "How Egyptians Toppled Mubarak—and Who Will Lead Them Now," *Christian Science Monitor*, February 12, 2011. |
| Vivian Salama | "The Dashed Revolution," *Newsweek*, January 25, 2013. |
| Emad El-Din Shahin | "Brutality, Torture, Rape: Egypt's Crisis Will Continue Until Military Rule Is Dismantled," *Guardian*, March 5, 2014. |
| Lee Smith | "Egypt Against Itself: A Society on the Edge of Chaos," *Weekly Standard*, February 18, 2013. |
| Peter James Spielmann | "Rights Group: Egypt Coup Stuns Democracy Trend," Associated Press, January 23, 2014. |

OPPOSING
VIEWPOINTS®
SERIES

CHAPTER 3

# What Political, Economic, and Social Policies Should Egypt Adopt?

# Chapter Preface

The Muslim Brotherhood was founded in 1928 by an Egyptian political activist and schoolteacher, Hassan al-Banna, who was concerned that Islamic principles were being trampled by Egypt's modernization and secularization. Initially, the group focused on charitable activities, such as expanding access to medical care and education in rural areas and promoting Islamic values. The Muslim Brotherhood grew rapidly, and by the late 1930s had taken root in every Egyptian province. By 1940, it had attracted more than a half million members and had spread to other Arab countries.

At that time, Egypt was a monarchy ruled by King Farouk and a colony of the British Empire. A growing number of Egyptians were discontent with British colonial rule and began working to resist British domination. The Muslim Brotherhood was key to that effort. The group's long reach and history as a charitable organization gave it access to even remote areas and credibility among the lower middle classes. Banned from participating in parliamentary elections, the group's members began to embrace the idea of political resistance and activism. Some members began to push more radical methods—including terrorism—to force a decisive confrontation with the state.

The Muslim Brotherhood formed an alliance with the Free Officers, a group of nationalistic military officers with the same goals: rid Egypt of British influence and depose the monarchy. The ensuing revolution in 1952 succeeded, but resulted in a military takeover of the country. The Muslim Brotherhood's dream of a conservative Islamic state was dashed when the military junta established a secular, nationalistic government led by Gamal Abdel Nasser, a former military leader. The new government refused to allow the Muslim Brotherhood a bigger role in political matters and rejected the demand for a constitution based on Islamic law, not secular principles. The relationship between the two forces quickly soured.

In 1954 a failed assassination attempt against Nasser prompted the military regime to ban the Muslim Brotherhood and throw its leaders in jail. Over the next few years, thousands of members were questioned, imprisoned, and tortured. The repression of the Muslim Brotherhood led to an ideological shift in the group. In its early years, al-Banna had preached nonviolence and a focus on social welfare activities; however, political repression under the military regime had led to increasing radicalism and a willingness to use terrorist methods to achieve the group's goals of an Islamist state. Much of the Muslim Brotherhood's radical writings during this time have been cited as central influences on later radical Islamist groups, including al Qaeda.

Despite the ban of the Muslim Brotherhood, the group continued to wield significant influence with the public. Restrictions on the group were relaxed under the administration of Anwar Sadat, who realized the organization's widespread support and the value of working with its members to improve conditions in the country. His administration began to bring the group back into the mainstream.

By the 1980s, the Muslim Brotherhood was a political force in parliamentary elections in Egypt. It became the dominant political opposition in the country. The group's increasing success prompted a crackdown by government forces in the mid-2000s in an attempt to curb its growing influence.

After Hosni Mubarak was removed from office in 2011, the Muslim Brotherhood was in a prime position to gain political control of Egypt. The group's political wing, known as the Freedom and Justice Party, won the overwhelming majority of seats in the 2011–2012 parliamentary elections. Its presidential candidate, Mohamed Morsi, won the 2012 election.

The group's tremendous mainstream political success seemed to signal a golden era and a much anticipated opportunity to implement some of its long-held dreams of an Islamic state. However, a series of missteps by the Morsi administration and the public's growing mistrust of the Muslim Brotherhood's intentions and heavy-handed methods resulted in large demonstrations against the government. After a tense constitutional crisis was averted in 2013, Morsi was deposed by the Egyptian military on July 3, 2013. The Muslim Brotherhood was declared a terrorist organization later that year.

The future of the Muslim Brotherhood in Egypt is one of the topics examined in the following chapter, which considers the political, economic, and social policies that Egypt should adopt.

*"A secular political scene would not al-
low extremism to gain momentum."*

# Egypt Should Embrace Secular Governance

## Salma El Shahed

*Salma El Shahed is a student and political commentator. In the
following viewpoint, she advocates secular governance in Egypt,
viewing it as the best way to limit the power of government in
the lives of ordinary citizens. In her view, although it is impossible to completely separate religion and the state in her country,
a secular government would acknowledge the role of religion
without favoring one religion over another. Another advantage of
secular governance, she explains, is that it protects its citizens
from religious extremism, such as that posed by the Muslim
Brotherhood. She maintains that it is dangerous to have religious
leaders involved in civic leadership unless there are secular principles that effectively limit the damage such leaders can do to
vulnerable groups in society.*

As you read, consider the following questions:

1. What Egyptian politician reintroduced the Muslim
   Brotherhood into public life, according to the author?

2. According to the author, how is inheritance settled and divorces adjudicated in Egypt?

3. Which party does the author identify as the largest and most organized in Egypt?

I am a Muslim member of Egyptian society. I will vote for a government that protects a civil society, where creed, sex or colour do not determine our standard of living or how people treat one another.

The main reason I want a secular state is to limit the power of government. History shows that politicians play the religion card for their own purposes. For Egyptians the clearest example is Anwar Sadat's reintroduction of the Muslim Brotherhood into public life to rally support among the people in face of the leftist socialist opposition. Using the people's attachment to religion, he portrayed himself the pious leader as opposed to the secular commies. Although the Muslim Brotherhood was still banned from operating in public life while Sadat made use of it in this way, the fact that the Egyptian people uphold their religious beliefs strongly made his plan work.

One lesson to draw from this is that prevention is better than the cure. Extremists are an irregularity in every creed; they will always be present in public life and will always have some sort of support. A secular political scene would not allow extremism to gain momentum. There is nothing wrong with being religious, but politicians should not be allowed to capitalise on it.

## Conflicting Laws

On paper, the Arab Republic of Egypt has a secular constitution now, which is not based on any religious scriptures: No law dictates that the prime minister has to be of a certain faith. Every man and woman that is a member of this society has the freedom of worship, and in no way will be persecuted

## Islamic Secularism

Islamic secularism is a movement seeking to limit the scope of religious authority, parallel to similar movements in other faith traditions. The limitation may be ideological, as in secularist movements to remove religious authority from state institutions or from social relations; or it may be experiential, as in the encroachment by consumerism and mass media on activities previously regulated by religious authority. Ideological secularism arose in the nineteenth century, when atheists . . . rejected Islam as inherently incompatible with modern ideals of progress. In the twentieth century, ideological secularism gained adherents among devout progressives as well.

*Charles Kurzman, "Secularism, Islamic,"*
Encyclopedia of Islam and the Modern World.
*Ed. Richard C. Martin. Vol. 2. New York: Macmillan, 2004.*

against because of his or her religious beliefs. But there are laws that violate this, such as those requiring approval from the head of state to build a church, or not mentioning religion on official government identification cards.

In a civic state, society must accept that people have the God-given right to freedom of worship. However, Egyptians are a pious people. To an overwhelming majority, a marriage is obsolete if a man of God is not present to mark it. Inheritance in Muslim families is settled by sharia, and so are divorce settlements. But sharia cannot govern laws of international trade, or the laws of the Egyptian Football Association.

My secularism would prosecute a drunken man for driving under the influence rather than just drinking, and stop the construction of a church or a mosque because the construction site happens to be on a natural preserve. My secularism will ignore my choice to cover my hair or not while running for office, but pay attention to my actions and qualifications as a member of this collective society.

As a Muslim member of Egyptian society, I cannot adhere to the usual definition of secularism as a complete separation of church and state. My culture is too interwoven with religion: It is almost impossible to exclude religion from civic laws. But a state that is truly neutral between religions is something that we desperately need. One must make the distinction between religion and church. When a government abandons a church, it abandons the church's view of religion, rather than the religion itself.

I must live with the fact that the Muslim Brotherhood is today the largest and most organised political party in Egypt. But if they form the government, I want secular principles to limit its power. Although sharia law guarantees civic rights to non-Muslims, extremists can infiltrate the perhaps idealistic programs of spin-off parties such as the newborn Freedom and Justice Party [a political wing of the Muslim Brotherhood]. Previous religious leaders have proposed imposing the jizya poll tax [a tax on non-Muslim citizens], which is unheard of in a civic state. Egypt needs a secularism that will respect religion(s) but protect all its citizens.

> "In Egypt, arguably the most religion-obsessed country on earth, . . . we should not expect to see either genuine democracy or even its prerequisite, a strong degree of secularism, with or without the new constitution . . . anytime soon."

# Egypt Will Not Be a Truly Secular Country

*Raymond Stock*

*Raymond Stock is a translator, critic, biographer, and fellow at the Middle East Forum. In the following viewpoint, he investigates the background of Egyptian general and leader Abdel Fattah al-Sisi to find clues as to whether he will steer the country on a more secular path. Stock focuses on a research paper written by Sisi during his time studying at the US Army War College in 2006, in which he makes it clear that his view of democracy in Egypt would be built on Islam. Stock believes that Sisi and the military overthrew Egyptian president Mohamed Morsi because Morsi was more interested in abolishing any trace of secularist leadership and infusing Islamist law into every aspect of Egyptian society. Although Stock believes that Sisi will take*

*Egypt back in a secular direction, he suggests that Egypt will never be truly secular because religion and civic life are intertwined, a situation that has existed in Egypt since ancient times and will continue into the future.*

As you read, consider the following questions:

1. According to Stock, who succeeded Colonel Gamal Abdel Nasser as president of Egypt in 1970?

2. According to the viewpoint, when did Akhenaten, known as the "heretic king," rule Egypt?

3. What Nobel laureate in literature does the author identify as being born in Gamaliya, the old Islamic quarter of Cairo?

Egypt's new de facto pharaoh, General Abdel Fattah al-Sisi, is a man of mystery. Is he an Islamist, or a nationalist? Is he a person of high principle, or a lowly opportunist? And in a land which has known five thousand years of mainly centralized, one-man rule, with limited experience of democracy, when have we seen his type before, and where will he lead the troubled, ancient nation now?

## U.S. Response

These questions are crucial to knowing how the U.S. should react to al-Sisi's removal of Egypt's first "freely elected" president, Mohamed Morsi, on July 3 [2013] in answer to overwhelmingly massive street protests demanding that he do so, and to the ongoing bloody crackdown on Morsi's group, the Muslim Brotherhood (MB), that began on August 14. Citing the ongoing, actually two-way violence in Egypt, President Barack Obama's administration has now suspended much of our annual $1.6 billion aid to the country, save for money needed to maintain security operations along the Israeli border in Sinai and to directly support the 1979 Egypt-Israel peace treaty.

Earlier, the administration had stopped the scheduled delivery of four out of twenty F-16s to Egypt, cancelled the biannual "Bright Star" joint training exercises that had been set for September, and launched a review of the bilateral relationship. There has now been a delay in paying the final $585 million tranche of this year's aid package, pending that review, according to an October 9 report by the global strategic analysis firm Stratfor.

However, the administration has been careful not to classify Morsi's removal a "coup," which under U.S. law would require an immediate cutoff of *all* of our aid to Egypt. That assistance is vital to the U.S.'s favored access to the Suez Canal, maintenance of the 1979 Egypt-Israel peace treaty and crucial bilateral security cooperation against international terrorism. Nonetheless, the latest move puts the entire alliance at great risk, and plays into popular demands that Egypt switch to a more independent stance, or even adopt Russia as chief military supplier instead of the U.S., an idea made more enticing by Washington's apparent weakness in surrendering its interests in Syria to Moscow, and its seeming haste to make concessions to Cairo's post-MB regional antagonist in Tehran over the latter's nuclear program.

Yet along with a number of key congressional leaders and most of the mainstream media, Obama has been far more critical of al-Sisi and his use of force against a group that our government wrongly supported while in power under the illusion that it was "moderate," than they have been of the violence and mayhem of the MB.

Meanwhile, the MB's "peaceful demonstrators" have been busy burning scores of Christian churches and schools along with hundreds of Christian businesses while attacking other citizens, museums and public buildings, the police and the army, and waging an open war against the state in Sinai and around the country. As the total number of deaths in the past nearly two months of confrontations climbs toward the thousands, the MB clearly hopes to use its own "martyrs" (as both sides call their fallen) to generate sympathy for their unaltered goal of restoring Morsi to power. So far, however, it's not working. Despite a surge in turnout at demonstrations it organized to coincide with the state's grand celebrations of the 40th anniversary of the 1973 war on October 6, fewer and fewer people have been joining its protests, which have been tiny compared to the unprecedentedly huge demonstrations against the Islamists.

## The Secret Thesis

But what besides the obvious hard realities pushed al-Sisi to act when he did? What does he believe, and what does he want? A quiet man known for saying little and keeping his own counsel, in his year of study at the U.S. Army War College in 2006, al-Sisi produced a research paper or brief thesis on his views of Islam and the state. That document was first exposed by Robert Springborg, an expert on Egypt's military, in a July 28 article in *Foreign Affairs*.

Springborg predicted that al-Sisi, who has sworn to swiftly restore democracy after a nine-month transition, intends to keep real power for himself. Furthermore, Springborg warned of his "Islamist agenda," saying that he would not likely restore the "secular authoritarianism" practiced by Mubarak, but would install "a hybrid regime that would combine Islamism with militarism." Intriguingly, though it holds no state secrets, the document was classified, and was only released under a Freedom of Information Act request by Judicial Watch on August 8.

In it, al-Sisi declares, "There is hope for democracy in the Middle East over the long term; however, it may not be a model that follows a Western Template" (sic). By that, al-Sisi makes plain, he means that Middle Eastern democracy must be based not on secularism, but on Islam.

However, in an August 16 profile of the previously obscure general published by the Daily Beast by Mike Giglio and Christopher Dickey, those who know al-Sisi (few of whom will talk much about him) say that he grew up in a family that was both religiously conservative—not radical—but extremely nationalistic. And indeed it is that sense of nationalism which seems to have had the upper hand in motivating the actions he's taken thus far.

The chaos, economic calamity, and political upheaval that have rocked Egyptian society since a much more limited popular uprising against longtime president Hosni Mubarak resulted in Mubarak's ouster by the military on February 11, 2011 (at Obama's thinly veiled urging the night before)—and which led in part to al-Sisi's move against Morsi—have all been seen before.

## The Return of General Horemheb?

In 1952, the widespread corruption, resort to political assassination, and the burning of the most elegant parts of downtown Cairo (both of the latter done, it is thought, mainly by the MB) led a group of so-called Free Officers to overthrow Egypt's last king, the feckless Farouk—with covert aid from the U.S.—in a coup, and to declare a republic the next year. Though the move was clandestine and confined to the army, it gained massive popularity and created a mythic hero (who was really an epic failure), Colonel Gamal Abdel Nasser, the movement's charismatic leader, himself initially a mystery—and to whom al-Sisi is often compared today.

Or perhaps he will be more like Anwar Sadat, another Free Officer, who in 1970 succeeded Nasser—the father of one of Egypt's greatest military defeats, in the war of 1967. Sadat partially made up for Nasser's many economic and political blunders by launching a successful surprise attack against Israeli forces in Sinai in 1973 (though it culminated in yet another defeat), partially repealing Nasser's reckless state socialism, trading an alliance with the Soviet Union for one with the United States, and daring to make peace with Israel—though it cost him his life when Islamists shot him down on the anniversary of that "victory" in 1981.

Al-Sisi has rapidly returned to the direct and confident military cooperation with the Jewish state that Morsi reviles, in order to prevent al-Qa'ida-affiliated groups (believed to have cooperated with the Muslim Brotherhood) from staging deadly incidents along the sensitive border.

However, much less reassuringly, al-Sisi has begun to flirt with both Russia and China, and is known to have neither much affection for the U.S., or patience with Obama's pro-MB policy. But going back even further, to 1805, al-Sisi could turn out to be like Mohamed Ali Pasha—Farouk's first direct royal forebear, an Albanian-Kurdish mercenary who used popular discontent against Egypt's oppressive Ottoman governor to replace him in office.

Mohamed Ali would briefly revive Egypt's long-lost military glory, and more relevantly, would do so by breaking with his own patrons in Istanbul—a possible cautionary tale for Washington now. And yet, plumbing much more deeply the currents of Egyptian history, al-Sisi may really most resemble Horemheb, the last king of the fabled 18th Dynasty.

## An Ancient Story

Horemheb served as head of the army under Akhenaten (ruled 1353–1336 B.C.), the "heretic king" who became the first ruler of any country to embrace something close to monotheism, a fanatic who threw out the traditional pantheon of ancient Egyptian gods in favor of worship of the Aten, the disc of the sun. Akhenaten's navel-gazing neglect of the nation's economy and security while he persecuted the believers of other deities and—like Morsi—inserted his own followers everywhere in the bureaucracy, led to massive unrest and perhaps prompted his most trusted lieutenant, Horemheb, to overthrow him—though his exact fate is unknown.

Born a commoner, Horemheb did not seize the throne until its last royal claimant, Tutankhamun, had died—as well as the boy-king's aged tutor Ay, who had married his widow. But when he did take it, he promptly stamped out the hated Aten cult and brought back that of the suppressed Amun-Ra, leading to a century of initially strong and stable rule by people mainly bearing the name of his successor and military protégé, a man called Ramesses.

As a soldier, Horemheb was no doubt angry that Akhenaten allowed Egypt's hard-won empire in the Near East to largely slip away without a fight. The nation's sacred prestige fell for the first time in centuries, and had to be reestablished so that *ma'at*—meaning everything from truth to order to righteousness, bound up with Egypt's well-being—could reign once again. And that he quickly set out to do.

Here is a degree of parallel with al-Sisi, who reportedly had been enraged by Morsi's actions that led not only to a loss of Egypt's international prestige but also damaged her national sovereignty. This he saw not only in Morsi's apparent covert cooperation with militants who had killed and kidnapped many Egyptian troops in Sinai, but also in his release of numerous terrorists convicted of murdering their fellow Egyptians plus members of the army, police and foreign tourists. Two symbolic acts by Morsi also not only raised eyebrows, but a sense of alarm about his intentions.

## Morsi Set Off Alarms

The first was Morsi's decision not only to invite Tarek al-Zomor, a member of the terrorist organization, Al-Gama'a al-Islamiyya (the Islamic Group), who took part in the assassination of President Anwar Sadat on the eighth anniversary of his 1973 brief but psychologically crucial triumph over Israel in Sinai, but to place him in the front row during the commemoration of the day on October 6 last year. The second was Morsi's June 2013 appointment of Adel Mohamed al-Khayat, a leader of Al-Gama'a al-Islamiyya, which waged a civil war against the Mubarak regime in the 1990s, killing scores of foreign tourists as well as hundreds of security officials, politicians and Egyptian civilians, to be governor of Luxor—where its most violent attack killed 58 foreigners and four Egyptian police and tourist guides (who died trying to defend the others) in November 1997.

Moreover, in late June this year, Morsi threatened to declare jihad on the embattled Bashar al-Assad regime in Syria in which the military had no interest. Al-Sisi was similarly piqued that Morsi allowed some in his cabinet to make threats to attack a controversial dam in Ethiopia that it is feared will lessen Egypt's accustomed share of the Nile's vital waters. And he was reportedly appalled that Morsi had evidently even told Sudan's Islamist president, Omar al-Bashir, whom the U.N. [United Nations] has accused of genocide in Darfur, that he would consider giving that country land which lies in dispute between them on their common border.

To Egyptians since antiquity, to yield any part of the nation's territory is an unforgivable heresy.

## "But I Loved Egypt More"

Perhaps worst of all, the MB calls for the establishment of a new caliphate, and lately demanded that its capital be in Jerusalem, which would not only mean a war to the death with Israel for which Egypt is not prepared, but—if successful—would obliterate the nation's independence. . . .

Though the general wrote nostalgically in his U.S. [Army] War College paper of the caliphate that united the Islamic world for seventy years after the death of the Prophet Muhammad in 632, he stated as well that only extremists were calling for its immediate return now. And if it does come back, he would undoubtedly want it to be based in Cairo.

# The Ousting of President Morsi

In June of 2012, Mohamed Morsi became Egypt's first democratically elected president in the country's history. However, Morsi soon became unpopular among Egyptian citizens because he was a member of the Muslim Brotherhood, an Islamist political group, and was believed to be placing the group's objectives before the needs of the people. Though [Abdel Fattah al-]Sisi was not a member of the Muslim Brotherhood, he was a close associate of Morsi. In August of 2012, the president made him both the minister of defense and the commander in chief of Egypt's armed forces. The Egyptian people then began staging mass protests against Morsi, calling for his removal on the grounds that he had been neglecting responsibility toward anyone not associated with the Muslim Brotherhood.

On July 1, 2013, following months of riots and political unrest among Egypt's citizenry, Sisi warned the president that his actions would lead to his deposition by the military if he did not meet the demands of the populace. Sisi gave Morsi until July 3 to comply with the people's requests. When Morsi ignored this deadline and announced that he would not relinquish power, the Egyptian Army, led by Sisi, arrested Morsi and removed him and his Muslim Brotherhood–supported government from office. Sisi then announced the news to the people and named Adly Mansour as the interim president. Six days later, economist Hazem el-Beblawi became Egypt's interim prime minister.

*"Abdel Fattah al-Sisi,"*
*Gale Biography in Context. Detroit, MI: Gale, 2013.*

Adding to all this was Morsi's rapid and relentless attempt to turn Egypt into a one-party Islamist dictatorship, and how it had destroyed both tourism and foreign investment while turning formerly rather small, if persistent protests by scattered secularist groups in a historically pious society into the largest demonstrations the world had ever seen.

On October 8, the *Washington Post* ran an AP [Associated Press] story that quoted the first of a three-part interview of al-Sisi by the respected Egyptian daily *Al-Masry Al-Youm*, in which the general . . . recounts for the first time what led to his actions on July 3:

> [Al-Sisi] said the turmoil of the past three months could have been avoided if Morsi had resigned in the face of the protests that drew out millions against him, starting on June 30. Days after the protests began, [al-Sisi] said, he met with senior Brotherhood figures, including the group's strongman Khairat el-Shater.
>
> He said el-Shater warned him that the Brotherhood, which made up the backbone of Morsi's administration, would not be able to control retaliation by Islamic groups in Sinai and other areas if Morsi were removed.
>
> "El-Shater spoke for 45 minutes, vowing terrorist attacks, violence, killings by the Islamic groups," [al-Sisi] told the paper. "El-Shater pointed with his finger as if he is shooting a gun."
>
> He said el-Shater's speech "showed arrogance and tyranny," adding: "I exploded and said . . . 'What do you want? You either want to rule us or kill us?'"
>
> Addressing Islamists now in the wake of Morsi's fall, [al-Sisi] said, "Watch out while dealing with Egyptians. You have dealt with Egyptians as if you are right and they are wrong . . . (as if) you are the believer and they are the infidels. This is arrogance through faith."

In the first part of the interview published Monday, [al-Sisi] said he told Morsi in February, "your project has ended and the amount of antipathy in Egyptians' souls has exceeded any other regime." He added that the military's move against Morsi was driven by fears of civil war.

Given all this, could it be any wonder that the highly patriotic, if also pious general with whom Morsi had replaced the aged Mubarak holdover Mohamed Hussein Tantawi because of his seemingly solid Islamist credentials had—after long hesitation—eventually felt that he had to act for the sake of his country? Ironically, al-Sisi was born and raised in the old Islamic quarter of Cairo called Gamaliya, the native district of Egypt and the Arab world's first (and so far only) Nobel laureate in literature, Naguib Mahfouz (1911–2006).

Mahfouz, despite a very strict Islamic upbringing, was from his youth a pharaonist—someone who placed Egypt's unique national heritage above anything else, including Islam, in defining her identity—as well as his own. One of Mahfouz's most prescient works is his peculiar 1983 novel-in-dialogue, *Before the Throne*. In it he hauls about three score of the nation's rulers—from Menes in the First Dynasty to Sadat—before the Osiris Court, the divine tribunal which in ancient Egyptian belief judged the souls of the dead. *Before the Throne* features many cycles of tyranny, rebellion, chaos and restoration, which presage the events of the past three years in uncanny ways.

In the afterlife trial of Horemheb, there is an exchange between the general who turned on Akhenaten and the addled religious zealot himself that could well have taken place between al-Sisi and Morsi, though without the intense mutual affection, no doubt:

"I loved none of my followers more than you, Horemheb," Akhenaten reproached him. "Nor was I as generous with anyone as much as I was with you. My reward was that you betrayed me . . ."

"I deny nothing you have said," replied Horemheb. "I loved you more than any man I'd ever known—but I loved Egypt more." ...

## Reading the Tea Leaves

Time will tell if al-Sisi, currently calling the shots behind an all-secularist civilian government of technocrats of his choosing, is truly more nationalist than Islamist—whether he will restore *ma'at* or sharia (Islamic law)—and if he will guide Egypt back into stability (or fails to do so) as a democrat in uniform, or as a martinet behind a "democratic" curtain. A key clue will be if he pushes for a new constitution that omits the central problem with the one rammed through by Morsi, which not only made sharia the main source of legislation (as it was before)—but which also empowered the clerics of al-Azhar, the highest authority in Sunni Islam, to interpret all laws to ensure compliance with it.

A draft of the new constitution, released on August 21, would reinstate the Mubarak-era ban on religious parties, throw out the most offensive aspects of Morsi's Islamist constitution from the point of view of religious tolerance, and ban the formation of religious parties—a very good sign. The fifty-member commission (headed by former Arab League chief and presidential candidate Amr Moussa), that is now reworking the draft, in coordination with the panel of experts that produced it, may entirely rewrite the Morsi-era charter.

The only Islamist group to join the body and to play any part in the transition, the Salafi Al-Nour Party, has protested against the removal of the sharia provision—but the secularists, including the commission's spokesman, head of the Arab Writers Union Mohamed Salmawy, seem to control the process so far. However, the August 21 draft specifically outlawed the removal of the president by popular protest, reserving that right for Parliament (the lower house of which has been dissolved due to violations of elections laws since June 2012)—to the outrage of the activists who fought to bring down both Mubarak and Morsi.

A recent decree replaces the oath that members of the armed forces formerly took to the nation's president, constitution and laws with a declaration of loyalty solely to the country's military leadership. As the experience not only of Egypt both before and under the Brotherhood, but also Pakistan under its own generals, Gaza under Hamas and even Turkey under the more stealthily Islamist Recep Tayyip Erdogan has shown, only a separation of mosque and state with civilian control of the military can deliver anything like real democracy.

In Egypt, arguably the most religion-obsessed country on earth all through her world's-longest history (and one of the most authoritarian as well), we should not expect to see either genuine democracy or even its prerequisite, a strong degree of secularism, with or without the new constitution—or al-Sisi himself—anytime soon.

Yet at least Egypt will not be ruled by the MB—which threatens not only the world's oldest nation, but us all—thanks to this enigmatic character from the heart of Old Cairo: General Abdel Fattah al-Sisi.

> "The cynical use of religion to justify
> calculated political strategies is in fact
> disturbingly evident on both sides."

# Religious Figures Must Avoid Partisanship and Sectarianism

*Asma Afsaruddin*

*Asma Afsaruddin is an author and professor of Islamic studies at Indiana University in Bloomington. In the following viewpoint, she criticizes the cynical use of religion on both sides of the conflict in Egyptian politics. On one side, the military and its leader General Abdel Fattah al-Sisi were quick to justify the crackdown on the Muslim Brotherhood by associating some of the conservative Islamist beliefs of the group with terrorism; on the other side, the Muslim Brotherhood called for a revolt against the military regime and the establishment of a conservative Islamist state. In particular, the eagerness of prominent Muslim figures to take sides is troubling; as Afsaruddin points out, Muslim scholars have historically distanced themselves from partisan battles and have emphasized the importance of good governance above religious fanaticism. Afsaruddin argues that in order to build a just society based on the rule of law and good governance for all, re-*

*ligious figures must adhere to that traditional principle and abstain from destructive and divisive partisanship and sectarianism.*

As you read, consider the following questions:

1. According to the author, what two prominent religious figures in Egypt have come out in support of the ouster of Egyptian president Mohamed Morsi?

2. What Mongol ruler is said to have asked religious leaders in the thirteenth century about the qualities of a good leader?

3. What political theorist does the author identify as one who recognizes the validity of political rebellion?

Which side in Egypt is currently on the side of the angels?

We like to imagine that in any conflict (particularly political ones) the good guys can be easily separated from the bad guys; good guys play by the rules of the game, bad guys don't. Life is rarely that simple, of course, but the current situation in Egypt is especially complex. The cast of key characters keeps switching sides—villains have become heroes only to be rebranded as villains, and on and on.

Until the corpulent diva sings in the famous Cairo opera house, the political drama in Egypt is not over yet by a long shot.

## A Turbulent Situation in Egypt

The July [2013] military coup (for that is what it was) in Egypt has become one of the bloodiest military takeovers in recent history. Hundreds of civilians have been slain and thousands injured since the government led by [Mohamed] Morsi was overthrown by his former defense minister General [Abdel] Fattah al-Sisi.

Not too long ago, Morsi was elected to the presidency riding on the crest of popular support, reflecting massive relief on the part of the Egyptian people at [Hosni] Mubarak's ouster. The people had spoken loudly and clearly. But then things began to go awry—Morsi began to overreach and adopt unpopular legal measures without proper judicial oversight. The economy began to decline, attacks on Christian minorities increased and accusations of religious authoritarianism and corruption began to surface.

Once again large crowds of Egyptians, said to number in the millions, took to the streets—this time to register their disapproval of Morsi's government. The military claimed to derive a popular mandate from these massive demonstrations and moved in to overthrow the Morsi government, imprison the deposed president, and launch a murderous vendetta against members of the Muslim Brotherhood.

One might be justified in asking—are there *any* good guys left in this scenario? Even the Egyptian people who had won the world's admiration when they heroically rose up against the Mubarak government and enthusiastically participated in democratic elections now appears to have tarnished their image by rising up against the first democratically elected government in their history.

This has paved the way for violent military intervention in the political affairs of the country and resurrected old stereotypes about "Arab despotism."

## The Reaction from Religious Figures

The religious and moral rhetoric that has been deployed on all sides is equally confusing. Ali Jum'a, the chief jurisconsult (Grand Mufti) in Egypt and Ahmad al-Tayyib, the rector of Al-Azhar University, both appointed by former president Hosni Mubarak, have supported the military coup. In a legal opinion (*fatwa*) that has been widely disseminated on the Internet, Jum'a in particular has energetically endorsed the overthrow of Morsi and supported the bloody aftermath of the military takeover (a position he subsequently denied having taken on his official website). The governments of conservative Muslim countries, such as Saudi Arabia and the Persian Gulf countries, have supported the coup as well, anxious as they are about the democratic "contagion" spreading to their realms. The Gulf countries' embrace of the avowedly secular Egyptian military and the Azhar elite's support of the military coup unhinges the usual assumptions about religious and secular alliances in the Arab world.

Morsi's supporters largely drawn from the Muslim Brotherhood have also resorted to religious rhetoric to attempt to galvanize popular opposition to the military. They regard their political resistance as a justified *jihad* against the usurpation of power by the military in defiance of the democratic elections held in July 2012. Essam El-Erian, a prominent member of the Muslim Brotherhood, declared in the immediate aftermath of the coup that "we will continue the fight, jihad and struggle in a peaceful protest."

Where then should the moral and ethical lines be drawn, if at all? Can both sides be right or wrong at the same time?

It is clear that political allegiances are driving the current situation in Egypt, even though such allegiances are frequently cloaked in highly emotive religious idiom. Despite the charged religious rhetoric on both sides, at the end of the day, the principal actors in this unfolding tragedy are motivated mostly by political power.

Many of us who study Islamic thought have been taken aback by the eagerness with which specific religious scholars have taken sides in the current overheated political climate in Egypt. Traditionally, Muslim scholars tended to stay aloof from politics, leery of accepting government employment. Religious scholars in the medieval period usually derived their income from privately funded charitable endowments beyond the reach of the government. Consequently, they had the moral freedom to criticize the government. The situation changed dramatically during the period of European colonization and in the post-colonial period when these charitable endowments were dissolved and handpicked religious scholars were placed on the government payroll. This effectively turned them into spokespersons for the government; the stature of religious scholars as independent moral arbiters has never been the same.

Despite what some Washington pundits, like David Brooks, have remarked, the question to be posed now is not whether Egypt is ready for democracy or not—that ship has sailed. The relevant question is: Are Egyptians ready to uphold the rule of law regardless of the political consequences?

## Establishing a Just Society

The creation of just, ordered societies is in fact the primary objective of the Muslim political tradition—and Muslim scholars often took it upon themselves to promote this, sometimes even overriding religious considerations. The historian Ibn al-Tiqtaqa relates that when the Mongols had taken possession of Baghdad in the thirteenth century, their ruler Hulagu Khan is said to have assembled the religious scholars in the city and posed a loaded question to them: According to their law, which alternative is preferable—the disbelieving ruler who is just or the Muslim ruler who is unjust? After moments of anguished reflection, one well-known scholar took the lead by signing his name to the response, "the disbelieving ruler who is just." Others are said to have followed suit in endorsing this answer.

Was this a politically expedient response? Perhaps. But there is no denying that this scholarly position highlights the importance of justice as the hallmark of a well-ordered polity in Islamic political thought, regardless of the religious affiliation or attitudes of the ruler. Morsi and his supporters should not have assumed that by simply proclaiming their Islamic

## Religion and Geopolitics

Religion and politics have been intertwined and used as a source of temporal power since ancient times. More than 4,500 years ago, the ancient Egyptians and Sumerians revered rulers as gods or as god's representative on earth. There have been many rulers who have used a close association with religion to consolidate domestic power and justify foreign policy decisions, including combat. Today, religion forms the lens through which many geopolitical issues, including terrorism, regional conflict, and even foreign trade, are viewed.

The existence of state religion is the most obvious example of the relationship between religion and politics. A state religion is a religious body or doctrine that is endorsed by the government. Many beliefs that once existed as state religion—for example, the gods endorsed by city-states Egypt, Sumer, and Greece to Zoroastrianism in Persia—have been largely relegated to the annals of history.

*"Religion and Geopolitics," Global Issues in Context*
*Online Collection. Detroit, MI: Gale, 2014.*

credentials they could paper over their ineffective policies and judicial high-handedness and continue to rally the majority of Egyptians to their side. Rhetoric does not substitute for actual accomplishments on the ground.

## Religion as a Weapon

The cynical use of religion to justify calculated political strategies is in fact disturbingly evident on both sides. Al-Sisi and his allies have declared Morsi's supporters to be "terrorists" guilty of inciting violence against the government, drawing a ready equation between Islamism and terrorism. Emboldened by the top religious leaders' support for the coup as protecting the larger common good, the military government continues its campaign to hunt down and slay their opponents with impunity. The subsequent human toll to date has been described by Human Rights Watch as "the most serious incident of mass unlawful killings in modern Egyptian history."

Certain members of the Muslim Brotherhood on the other hand claim to be carrying out a "jihad" against the military government and have been willing to register their moral outrage by risking death at the hands of the army.

Well-established Islamic political thought and history would prove both sides to be abusing Islamic legal terminology. From the viewpoint of classical scholarship, Muslims do not wage *jihad* against one another; the military form of it was reserved for external aggressors only.

As for the broader understanding of jihad as a moral and social struggle, such an endeavor must not lead to loss of innocent civilian lives or foment "social dissension"—*fitna* in Arabic—condemned in Islamic ethical literature as morally reprehensible. On this latter point, Jum'a in his support for the coup as an expression of majority popular will may appear to be right. But it should be noted at the same time that classical jurists and political theorists like [Abu al-Hasan] al-Mawardi (d. 1058) also recognized the validity of political rebellion.

Nowhere in the political literature is the ruler granted the right to annihilate his political opponents because he disagrees with their position.

## A Place for Dissent

Unless these rebels have resorted to proven violent acts of brigandage and sedition—which would place them in a different category of miscreants—they are *not* to be put to death. Instead they are entitled to a fair hearing before jurists—they cannot be indicted simply through the legal pronouncements of recognized religious scholars or in the "court" of public opinion. Despite the attempts of conservative scholars to idealize political quietism and conformity—sometimes at the expense of justice and fair political representation—there has always been a place within Islamic political and intellectual history for reasoned dissent. As Muhammad is reported to have said: "In difference there is mercy for my community."

The freewheeling misuse of religion on both sides is a dismal augury of continued social and political chaos in Egypt. Time and time again, revolutionaries have eventually learned that without the rule of law and principled adherence to justice, the popular will does not translate into a moral mandate for positive social and political change. Religion can be an important ally in this process but only if it does not degenerate into a handmaiden to the pursuit of rank political power.

> *"It was ironic that the vast masses of people who gathered in Tahrir Square to press for freedom and equality could not tolerate the outcome of their own demands."*

# The Egyptian Government Must Be Inclusive to Islamist Factions

## Anando Bhakto

*Anando Bhakto is a political reporter. In the following viewpoint, he suggests that the overthrow of democratically elected president Mohamed Morsi and the banning of the Muslim Brotherhood are detrimental to the establishment of a stable Egyptian state. Bhakto contends that the military coup in Egypt dealt a severe blow to many across the Arab world who believed that there could be a constructive partnership between democracy and Islam. He reports that a number of security experts believe that radical Islamist groups will turn to violence to make their voices heard and to gain power in Egypt. It would be in the country's best interest to reconsider its oppression of the Muslim Brotherhood for the sake of a lasting peace.*

As you read, consider the following questions:

1. According to Bhakto, who is the founder of the Muslim Brotherhood?

2. What Muslim Brotherhood leader does the author identify as the one who brought the group into the political process? .

3. What Egyptian militant group claimed responsibility for an attack against Mohammed Ibrahim's house on September 5, 2013?

Whether or not the Arab Spring heralded a democratic transition in the Arab world, it was significant in the sense that even political parties with a predominantly Islamic ideology took to the streets demanding justice and fair elections rather than a state based upon sharia.

Although many argue that the Muslim Brotherhood only joined the revolts at later stages in Egypt, the organization became an important force pressing for the formation of a civilian government.

However, [Mohamed] Morsi's undemocratic expulsion from power, supported and executed by Egypt's military generals, and his current trial for charges of inciting violence and murder—charges that are more political than legal—serve as a reminder to Islamist groups that more often than not they will be treated as outcasts within a political setup. The recent designation of the Muslim Brotherhood as a "terrorist group" is also a case in point.

This in turn stands to thwart the very experiment of political Islam—the marriage between Islam and democracy—which some experts had believed would democratize much of the region in the long run.

For decades, Islamist organizations had been in two minds over whether to join the mainstream electoral process or mobilize people as a non-state organization through civil society initiatives and social services. They hoped the latter method would help them secure support of the masses and put them in a position to replace the existing Western-inspired parliamentary system of governance with an Islamic caliphate in the future.

## Al-Banna and the Muslim Brotherhood

This ambiguity had its origins in Hassan al-Banna, the founder of the Muslim Brotherhood, who was critical of Western concepts of justice and democracy. Strongly influenced by and opposed to the sweeping impact of British colonialism on Egyptian life and culture, unlike other Muslim groups in Egypt in the 1920s and 1930s, the Brotherhood believed Islam was sufficient to counter foreign domination.

For al-Banna, Islam was "complete and all-embracing, governing all aspects of private and public life. . . . Islam was but politics, society, economy, law and culture." It was, therefore, deviation from Islam and the subsequent imitation of Western customs that weakened Egyptian society. Thus, the replacement of sharia by man-made laws of the West was not just cultural surrender but, more importantly, an act of heresy.

Nevertheless, al-Banna strongly believed in and advocated for Islamization from below, a process involving *da'wa* (preaching) that aimed at creating an Islamic government as the natural and gradual consequence of peaceful Islamization.

## The Use of Violence

However, later down the line, leading Muslim Brotherhood member Sayyid Qutb legitimized the use of violence and soon armed Islamist groups extended their violent actions against domestic targets. Qutb argued:

> "Islamization from below is too slow a process impeded by the intervention of local authorities and foreign powers. Therefore, the only solution lies in the concepts of takfir

and jihad. True Muslims are obligated to overthrow and kill such rulers in order to establish an Islamic state."

After an initially inclusive policy towards the Brotherhood—as for example witnessed by the inclusion of Ahmed Hosni and Ahmed Hassan el-Bakoury into the Egyptian government—then president Gamal Abdel Nasser led a crackdown against the group. This was related to the Brotherhood's refusal to disband its paramilitary wing, *al-jihaz al-sirri*, and an unsuccessful assassination attempt on Nasser's life by a Muslim Brother in 1954.

Consequently, the group was formally banned, thousands of its activists were incarcerated and many were executed. By the late 1960s, the Brotherhood realized that if it were to ever reemerge in the political scene, it could only be possible by abandoning its radical positions. The organization, therefore, turned to nonviolent resistance which included societal reform and spreading Islamic education at the grassroots level.

This crystallized into some sort of marriage or understanding between Islam and democracy, in that the Brotherhood realized it was possible to push for their Islamic agendas by becoming a part of the existing political system.

The Muslim Brotherhood, under the leadership of their third mentor Umar al-Tilmisani, joined the political process. Al-Tilmisani paved the way for the Brotherhood's participation in the 1984 elections in alliance with the neo-Wafd [party], and in 1987 they formed a coalition with the Workers party.

## Political Islam, Violent Struggle, and the Egyptian Military

Egypt's Muslim Brotherhood undertook widespread reforms in order to widen their social base and enter the electoral process. They were, however, bitterly criticized by more radical Islamist organizations, such as al-Qaeda, which asserted that proponents of political Islam would be treated as outcasts within a democratic setup, and that it was only through violent struggle that Islam could find its rightful place in society.

The Egyptian military has potentially strengthened the appeal of those in favor of armed struggle in the Islamist camp by ousting Morsi.

Significantly, Islamists in other Muslim countries, especially those characterized by a lack of transparent and democratic institutions, have also met the same fate as the Brotherhood.

Algeria is a prime example of this development. After the Islamic Salvation Front (FIS) surged to victory in the first round of the 1991 elections, the Algerian military overturned the result and led a violent crackdown on Islamists. The country slid into a protracted civil war for over ten years, as a result.

In Turkey, before the later electoral success of the Justice and Development Party (AKP), the Islamists were driven out of power in 1997 by a soft coup enacted by the country's military against then prime minister Necmettin Erbakan, barely two years after they were democratically elected to office.

## An Inherent Antagonism Between Democracy and Islam?

Such incidents strengthened the radical Islamists' belief that an inherent antagonism between democracy and Islam exists, and that political Islam is irrelevant and inconsequential.

In Egypt, the Brotherhood were victorious on three occasions: they won the parliamentary elections in 2011–2012; the presidential elections in 2012; and when they sought a two-round referendum for the 2012 constitution drafted by an Islamist-dominated Constituent Assembly, they once again polled a staggering 63.8% of the popular vote.

But with successive humiliation at the hands of Egypt's judiciary and the military, ranging from the dissolution of Par-

© Steve Greenberg/Cartoonstock.com.

liament to an unabashed *coup d'état*, the Brotherhood is under mounting pressure from fellow Muslim organizations to give up its experiment with democracy.

For example, Ansar al-Sharia of Libya said the Muslim Brotherhood of Egypt was wrong by participating in elections to gain power and criticized its failure to implement sharia. The Somali Islamist group al-Shabaab voiced similar criticism.

Al-Qaeda leader Ayman al-Zawahiri remarked that the coup testified Islamic rule cannot be established through democracy, while he urged all Islamists to adopt a policy of violent opposition to the ruling elite. This alternative path threatens to render the Brotherhood more ideologically driven than it is now as a political organization, which believes Islamic objectives can be achieved by gradual transformation of society.

If, however, the Brotherhood commits itself to attaining the Islamic objectives through coercion, it is likely to become more exclusive and intolerant.

## Morsi's Ouster: A Severe Blow to the Islamist Agenda

Indeed, Morsi's ouster was a severe blow to the Islamist agenda across the Arab world, which aimed at bringing about some sort of marriage between democracy and Islam. For many, it has created the impression that secular and liberal opposition parties are leading a personal vendetta against the Brotherhood and that they would never allow it to run a government.

The Brotherhood is already beginning to read the current struggle as an existential battle against the Egyptian military. Now that they have been designated as a "terrorist group," it is doubtful if they will ever again get the chance to participate in the electoral process as a free, democratic entity.

It was ironic that the vast masses of people who gathered in Tahrir Square to press for freedom and equality could not tolerate the outcome of their own demands. Some experts believe that Egypt's elite and business classes, together with the media which is more responsive to this affluent class, were perturbed to see the Brotherhood's rise to power on the ballot of the poor, illiterate, and other marginalized sections of society—with which the elites have traditionally had little interaction.

For them, the Muslim Brotherhood was the representative of the deprived classes and, therefore, lacked the intellectual caliber to make decisions on matters relating to administration or governance, which was likely to also impact the sensibilities of the rich and upper-middle class.

## Embracing Violence

According to Hayat Alvi, associate professor in national security affairs, US Naval War College, Egypt now faces a real danger of Islamist militancy. In an interview the author conducted with her in August 2013, she said:

"We see evidence of a growing violent insurgency, which might reach full-fledged status at some point, with recent car bombs, rail bombs, and assassination attempts. There is more of that to come. I contend that the real Islamist militancy danger lies with the Salafis who have now aligned themselves with the [Abdel Fattah al-]Sisi–backed coup regime. The Muslim Brotherhood can cause a lot of trouble and violence, but the Salafis are even more hard-line in their Islamism.... So, Egypt will face layers of Islamist militant networks vying for power, carrying out attacks against the government and security forces and other targets, and triggering a massive exodus of educated professional Egyptians, leading to a huge brain drain. That's my prediction."

Moreover, Michael Hughes, a columnist at the *Huffington Post*, told the author:

"If the military continues to repress the Muslim Brotherhood and disallows it from participating politically, it will most certainly come back to haunt Egypt because it will only fuel the extremist cause."

Importantly, there has been an increase in attacks in Egypt targeting ministers and other public officials in the aftermath of the coup. Although Sinai-based militant group Ansar Bayt al-Maqdis claimed responsibility for the attack against Interior Minister Mohammed Ibrahim's house on September 5, 2013, and while the Muslim Brotherhood has so far remained nonviolent, the attack suggests that coercive measures against the Brotherhood will incite such violent reactions from individual Islamist groups, which in turn may revive a 1990s-like insurgency in Egypt.

"The events of the past few months were bound to create a sentiment among [the] wider Islamist community that the injustice they are experiencing should be fought," said Issandr El Amrani, North Africa project director at the International Crisis Group.

## Muslim Brotherhood: No Inclination to Take Up Arms

However, it would be premature to compare these sporadic attacks to the insurgency of the 1990s, more so when the Brotherhood has limited its role to street protests and has not shown an inclination to take up arms even in the face of the deadliest military crackdown. The Brotherhood understands that a violent resistance will not only unite the opposition against them, but it will also give the armed forces a ready pretext to unleash more coercive measures.

Al-Sharif Nassef, editor at the *Egyptian Gazette*, who the author spoke to last month, was hopeful that the Brotherhood would continue in electoral politics, should they be allowed:

> "According to Professor Nathan Brown, who I spoke with recently, it is unlikely that the Brotherhood will formally take up arms. However, there remains the possibility that former Brotherhood supporters, relatives of those arrested or killed during the crackdown, and disenfranchised Islamists will try and subvert progress through random acts of violence. The intelligence and security apparatuses are, at the moment, too well-equipped and too powerful for any meaningful insurgency to break out."

While there is no doubt that the Brotherhood overreached its power while in office, excluded large segments of Egyptian society from the constitution-writing process and completely failed at economic policies, the coup was ill-conceived.

Experts believe that the Muslim Brotherhood would have been defeated in the next parliamentary elections under the weight of their own misgovernance. That would have compelled them to become more inclusive and secularize their political agendas.

The same happened in Turkey where the ruling Islamist AKP agreed to compromise on its policies. It declared Islam as the official religion of the state but stopped short of making any attempt to validate Islamic law.

In Egypt, the military coup and the subsequent outlawing of the Brotherhood have left no room for such transformation. If anything, it has abetted the Muslim Brotherhood's possible degeneration into an underground force outside of the political process.

> "The problem is that politicians and in-
> tellectuals in Egypt avoid discussing the
> most important issue in their country,
> which is the economy."

# Economic Reform, the Only Way Forward for Egypt

*Jamal Khashoggi*

*Jamal Khashoggi is a journalist, columnist, and author. In the following viewpoint, he identifies one of the main causes of the Egyptian revolution to be the country's deteriorating economy. Khashoggi contends that politicians want to deny the economy's central role in the political and social strife that has roiled Egypt for the past three years because they know that it will require painful and difficult solutions. At issue is the country's increasing budget deficit and the sharp cuts to the public sector that are vital to address it—solutions that will be hugely unpopular with the public. Khashoggi recommends that Egyptian leaders look to the examples of Chile and Turkey to reform the Egyptian economy with the goal of injecting the principles of a free market system. Khashoggi maintains that such significant reforms would mean that there would be harsh consequences for some people in the short term, but in the long term, all Egyptians would reap the benefits.*

As you read, consider the following questions:

1. According to Khashoggi, what Egyptian president attempted to make economic policy under his "Open Door" policy?

2. How much is the Egyptian budget deficit, according to the author?

3. What Nobel laureate economist does the author identify as the influence on economic reforms in Chile during the 1970s?

Supporters of Egyptian field marshal Abdel Fattah al-Sisi like to picture him as another Gamal Abdel Nasser. However, he certainly knows that if he wants to succeed as Egypt's president, he should never be like Abdel Nasser, rather he should fix the Egyptian economy that was tarnished by the "eternal leader." He certainly knows that Egypt's problem is the economy and that all those who came after Abdel Nasser tried to rebuild the economy but did not succeed.

President Anwar Sadat tried to make economic reforms under his "Open Door" policy, without compromising the structure of the rentier state and the command economy left by Abdel Nasser. The result was the emergence of a parallel economy producing what the Egyptians called "fat cats" who enjoy prosperity alone, away from the underprivileged majority. Hosni Mubarak made better achievements by hiring qualified economists, but the reality of a parallel economy continued. Mubarak once justified it using the "Trickle Down Economy", a theory that became popular in the United States during the era of former U.S. president Ronald Reagan, who encouraged reducing taxes on rich people and giving incentives to businessmen, hoping to increase their incomes and thus affect the rest of the economy.

It is clear that this theory failed in Egypt and subsequently caused the Jan. 25 revolution, the most important slogan of which was "social justice". The problem is that politicians and intellectuals in Egypt avoid discussing the most important issue in their country, which is the economy. They prefer to deal with any other issue such as discussing whether the state is civil or religious, civil or military, military or "Brotherhood". They also waste time discussing international conspiracies and "revolutionary" treatments for HIV and hepatitis. They would rather debate anything but the economy, perhaps because they all know that it is the real monster that can only be taken on through very painful decisions that may lead to a revolution, much bigger than what Egypt witnessed in the past three years. All the economic reforms made by previous Egyptian governments were mere tranquilizers and unfulfilled promises. The most important reason for the resignation of Hazem el-Beblawi's government days ago was that it issued a decision to raise the minimum wage that had been implemented in January, but it did not include everyone. Those who were included did not enjoy the raise due to burgeoning inflation. Consequently, factional strikes and sit-ins spread across the country.

## The Difficult Solution

Any future president of Egypt knows that the problem is simple but its solution is very difficult. The problem is that the state's income is less than its spending; the Egyptian budget deficit is about 240 billion pounds ($34.9 billion), equivalent to 14 percent of Egypt's GDP during the last fiscal year, and the only possible solution is that these two numbers should at least be equal. This will only be possible by getting rid of Abdel Nasser's legacy: the massive public sector, an army of unnecessary employees with more than six million employees who are expected to increase to seven million soon with the government's offer of permanent contracts for the temporary staff. This week, 75,000 teachers were offered permanent contracts, while the state subsidizes the prices of costly commodities, most notably energy which alone needs 140 billion pounds (20 billion dollars) from the state budget, along with the complex network of "protective" systems that restricted the economy and kept Egypt caught between a free market economy and a command economy.

During Mubarak's term, they tried to address these issues, but the solutions were marred by corruption and exclusions. Despite being "unfair" for a lot of people, it helped in achieving good growth rates for the Egyptian economy overall, recording 7.1 percent growth during the peak of the global financial crisis in 2008; however a quarter of the Egyptian population living below the poverty line did not benefit from it. Despite all that, this is very good news compared with the growth rate during the first quarter of the current fiscal year, which did not exceed one percent.

Many countries have faced the same situation as Egypt, but "President" Sisi should look into two particular cases while reading and examining the changes that led them to get out of the bottleneck; it was not easy but rather expensive. As long as Egypt is paying an expensive price to impose security and restore the state's respect for an individual-based regime, we cannot advise him to expand his national base through reunification and reconciliation; it is better to use this cost to serve the nation and not the individual, so that it won't be a vicious cycle of another crisis but an opportunity to break the cycles of totalitarian rule to establish an economic renaissance for a pluralistic democratic society.

## Taking Note

The above mentioned two cases are Chile and Turkey, where chaos and inflation prevailed for decades, to the point that the army was prompted to intervene. Judging if it was praiseworthy or blameworthy does not matter now. In Chile, General Pinochet came to power in 1971 and ousted the elected government. He was very tough, to the extent that Chileans are

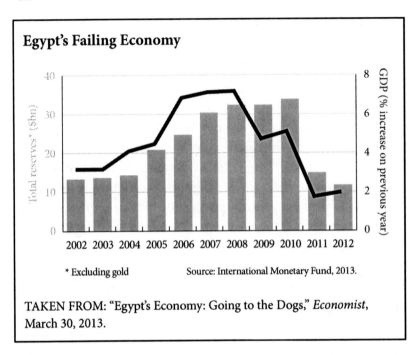

## Egypt's Failing Economy

* Excluding gold          Source: International Monetary Fund, 2013.

TAKEN FROM: "Egypt's Economy: Going to the Dogs," *Economist*, March 30, 2013.

still imprinted by the memories of his harsh years. Thousands are still missing. The current president's father died after being tortured in Pinochet's prisons, but most of them admit that he succeeded in imposing economic reforms that his elected predecessors have failed to achieve. Thus, he paved the way for what is known today as the "Miracle of Chile". Even more, Chilean students of famous Nobel laureate economist Milton Friedman, led the economic reform in their country during the Pinochet era, applying Friedman's theory regarding the "free market", which led—according to what he says in his memoirs—to a "better performance in the economy, saving Chile from the central government and replacing the ruling military class with a democratic society". Perhaps some Egyptian liberals would find better justification for accepting the development of the "on hold" democracy if they went through the ideas of the Milton Friedman school that is also known as "neoliberalism". The theory believes that democracy works best in self-sustaining communities that enjoy a free economy.

The Egyptian society is certainly not self-sustained on the economic level and does not enjoy a free economy, but one of the main challenges faced by the "neoliberals" in Eastern Europe and Russia is the corruption and abuse of the "minority" or what is known as the "oligarchy", who now control the destiny of the country. President Vladimir Putin confronts them at times and lets them be at other times, they have not decided on the terms of their relationship with the state yet. Egyptian elites must recognize the existence of the "oligarchy" in their country, forming centers of power involved in the governance of the country, and they should admit as well that this case cannot be sustained under a fully democratic regime.

In Turkey, General Kenan Evren led a military coup in 1980 against an elected government after years of chaos. In the first two years of his term as president, Turkey saw dark days; tens of thousands of detentions and executions and like Chile, Turkish people are still searching for thousands of missing Turks. He then handed the presidency to economist Turgut Özal, who led the massive economic reforms related to the "neoliberal" school, opening the door for historic reconciliation between Turkey's secular Kemalist legacy and its Islamic heritage. A decade later, the military rule withdrew, paving the way for an economic miracle in Turkey. In the end, the rulers left and Turkey and Chile remained. They have even topped the list of the fastest growing economies. Today, any Turkish or Chilean citizen can be sitting in an elegant restaurant, reading a newspaper that is freely criticizing or praising the government, and he can be discussing with his friend the upcoming elections in his country without being afraid of national security or being worried if he can pay the luxurious restaurant's bill.

Egyptians should base their heated arguments on the economic dilemma. They should accept harsh solutions that would be better taken under a national consensus, unfortunately that needs a miraculous reconciliation that does not seem in sight. The only one who did that is novelist Ezzedine Choukri Fishere in his wonderful "prophetic" novel *Exit Door*, which opened all the doors except the exit door. I reference Ezzedine Fekri's character who comes to power, defeats all of his opponents in order to achieve the goals of the revolution, but fails when addressing the country's six million employees. The bureaucracy monster symbolizes the rentier state, perhaps because he was alone.

*"Since the most recent wave of protests began in Tahrir Square on June 30 [2013], there have been 186 recorded sexual assaults."*

# Egypt's Rape Culture Must Be Confronted and Not Used for Political Gain

*Anna Lekas Miller*

*Anna Lekas Miller is a journalist. In the following viewpoint, she reports that sexual violence has increased dramatically since the Egyptian revolution. In Tahrir Square, the public square in Cairo known as the center of the revolutionary protests, hundreds of thousands of women have been groped, stripped, beaten, and raped. Disturbingly, there have been no prosecutions of the attackers. Miller notes that women in Egypt are often blamed for wearing provocative clothing, being immodest, or for just being around men in public. Some authorities have used the reports of sexual violence for political advantage. She points to the Muslim Brotherhood who, when in power, smeared government protesters as thugs, rapists, and misogynists. In the West, Islam is often blamed as the cause for the rise in sexual violence in Egypt.*

*Miller argues that Egypt's rape culture should not be used for political gain but should be addressed by well-considered policies and motivated by concern and respect for women and their safety.*

As you read, consider the following questions:

1. According to a recent survey by UN Women, what percentage of Egyptian women report being sexually assaulted?

2. According to a 2008 survey with the Egyptian Center for Women's Rights, what percentage of Egyptian men believe that a woman's clothing choice invites harassment?

3. What American author was accused of a bias against Islam when she linked the religion with sexual harassment, according to Miller?

Since the most recent wave of protests began in Tahrir Square on June 30 [2013], there have been 186 recorded sexual assaults—including eighty the night that former president Mohamed Morsi was overthrown. Many of these attacks are mob-style sexual assaults, often involving between fifty and 100 assailants, in which a woman is surrounded, stripped, groped and in some cases beaten and gang-raped until she needs medical attention. And in some recent cases, women were attacked and penetrated with knives and other weapons.

In Egypt, they call this the "Circle of Hell."

Since the Egyptian revolution began more than two and a half years ago, hundreds of thousands of women have been sexually assaulted in Tahrir Square. And over the past two and a half years, not a single assailant of the thousands who participated in hundreds of attacks has been prosecuted.

"These men attack women because they know they can get away with it," said Yasmine, an Egyptian activist who doesn't wish to give her last name.

Many of the women surveyed agree that sexual violence has gotten worse since former president Hosni Mubarak was overthrown. Up until the most recent wave of protests, during which the Muslim Brotherhood pointed to sexual assaults in Tahrir Square in an attempt to delegitimize antigovernment opposition, the rampant attacks that happened under President Morsi's leadership have gone largely ignored.

## A Pervasive Problem

According to a recent survey from UN Women [also known as the United Nations Entity for Gender Equality and the Empowerment of Women], 99.3 percent of all Egyptian women report being sexually harassed, and 91.5 percent have experienced unwelcome physical contact. The country has three laws in the penal code that address sexual harassment, assault and rape—and though the punishments range from fines to imprisonment, including life sentences and the death penalty, these laws are rarely enforced. Instead, most women are discouraged from reporting their sexual assaults to the authorities. For most, the high risk of shame and humiliation in publicly outing oneself as a sexual assault survivor—and the assumption that one is tainted or, if unmarried, now unfit for marriage—far exceeds the likelihood that the assailant will be held accountable.

Like in the West, women's attire is often blamed for attacks, particularly Western-style clothing that many conservative Egyptians claim attracts assailants and in some cases even justifies rape. According to a 2008 survey with the Egyptian Center for Women's Rights, 53 percent of all men believe that a woman invites harassment through what she is wearing. Many of the women surveyed agree.

Despite these stereotypes, a woman's clothing doesn't have much bearing on the likelihood of an attack. One of the most famous photographs of the recorded history of Egypt's sexual assault epidemic is of a woman sprawled on the floor in only her blue bra, her traditional niqab veil ripped and shredded next to her after her attack.

## Egypt's Rape Culture

Although sexual harassment has always been widespread in Egypt, it is only recently that the word "taharrush," meaning "harassment" in Egyptian Arabic, has come into the popular lexicon. Before that, the word, "mu'aksa" meaning "flirtation" was used to describe these advances—even when they were nonconsensual. And under the leadership of President Mohamed Morsi and the Muslim Brotherhood, Egypt's rape culture has only become more entrenched.

For instance, after a wave of sexual assaults in Tahrir Square during the November 2012 demonstrations, several members of the Human Rights Committee of the Shura Council—the upper house of Parliament which, under Morsi's administration, held significant legislative powers—openly stated that women were "100 percent" responsible for their rapes by placing themselves in "such circumstances"—in other words, being in the square. Abu Islam, a prominent Islamic cleric and popular Egyptian television guest, expressed a similar view when he claimed, on national TV, that blaming a man for committing sexual assault was akin to "blaming a cat for eating meat that was left out." Reda Al-Hefnawy of the Muslim Brotherhood's Freedom and Justice Party went so far as to say that the women were to blame for the sexual assaults because they had violated the men's modesty.

## Finding a Political Advantage

As recently as March, the Muslim Brotherhood claimed that a United Nations declaration draft to end all violence against women would lead to the denigration of society. However, during the most recent wave of sexual assaults the Muslim Brotherhood finally paid attention to the attacks—not to condemn endemic violence against women but to exploit it for political gain. They pointed to the assaults—most of which occurred in Tahrir Square, the home base of the anti–Muslim Brotherhood protests—to delegitimize the opposition.

Immediately after the news of the first sexual assaults, a Muslim Brotherhood television channel, Misr 25, began a smear campaign against the protesters, calling them "thugs" and denouncing the way the "revolutionaries" treated women in Tahrir Square. The Brotherhood never once asked what they could do to help the survivors, and condemnation of the assaults was always framed within a condemnation of the anti-Morsi opposition.

The Muslim Brotherhood wasn't alone in leveraging the attacks for a political agenda. In the West, several commentators jumped on the latest wave of attacks as a means to criticize Islam and Arab culture. American novelist Joyce Carol Oates tweeted:

> Where 99.3% of women report having been sexually harassed & rape is epidemic—Egypt—natural to inquire: what's the predominant religion?

Oates was, of course referring to Islam—and the fact that between 80 and 90 percent of the Egyptian population identifies as Muslim.

Oates's tweets—which continued in the same vein—were decried by many as Islamophobic for their correlation of rape culture with religious culture. Her insinuation prompted the question does Islam also explain why one in four female college students in the US is sexually assaulted during their college career? Or why one in three female service members are sexually assaulted during their service in the US Army?

In Egypt as well as in the West, prominent responses to the waves of violence against women have failed to address the systematic causes and potential solutions to sexual assault. Instead, Islam itself has been scapegoated in the West, while in

Egypt the Muslim Brotherhood has blamed assaults on women's very presence in the square. And the [Supreme] Council of the Armed Forces and the interim leadership have remained silent on the assaults—even though they have now been ruling Egypt for over a month.

Although grassroots groups such as Tahrir Bodyguard and Operation Anti–Sexual Harassment (and Assault) have sent volunteers to patrol every demonstration and intervene in potential sexual assaults since their nascence during the November 2012 protests, the number of assaults has multiplied, not decreased. While many women say that these groups' presence makes them feel safer, these groups are still only protecting women from sexual assault, rather than addressing the root causes—a Band-Aid solution to a much greater problem.

As Egypt struggles under new leadership, Egyptian women, many of whom stood and fought alongside men during every phase of the revolution, are caught in a cross fire where their bodies are physically attacked and then their experience is exploited for political gain or as fodder for Islamophobia. Ultimately, this politicization—whether it is from the Muslim Brotherhood or Islamophobic American writers—is yet another powerful tool in convincing women to stay silent, thus perpetuating the cycle of sexual violence.

# Periodical and Internet Sources Bibliography

*The following articles have been selected to supplement the diverse views presented in this chapter.*

| | |
|---|---|
| Mohamad Bazzi | "Islamism After the Coup in Egypt," *Nation*, August 5–12, 2013. |
| Nathan J. Brown | "Grading Egypt's Roadmap Toward Democracy," *Foreign Policy*, May 5, 2014. |
| Mahmood Delkhasteh | "Egypt: Secular Dictatorship vs. Religious Dictatorship," *Huffington Post*, August 23, 2013. |
| Kevin Drum | "Most Egyptians Don't Want a Secular Government," *Mother Jones*, July 8, 2013. |
| Mohamad Elmasry | "Egypt's 'Secular' Gov Uses Religion as Tool of Repression," *Religion Dispatches*, April 29, 2014. |
| Shadi Hamid | "The Brotherhood Will Be Back," *New York Times*, May 23, 2014. |
| David D. Kirkpatrick | "Vow of Freedom of Religion Goes Unkept in Egypt," *New York Times*, April 25, 2014. |
| Heather Murdock | "Acts of New Government to Determine Fate of Political Islam in Egypt," *Voice of America*, May 26, 2014. |
| D. Parvaz | "Can Secularism Survive in Egypt?," *Al Jazeera*, April 9, 2013. |
| Richard Wike | "Egypt Isn't Stable," *Foreign Policy*, May 23, 2014. |
| Farid Zahran | "What Are the Political Factions Currently Operating Within Egypt?," *Daily News* (Egypt), August 30, 2013. |

OPPOSING
VIEWPOINTS®
SERIES

CHAPTER 4

# What Should Be US Policy on Egypt?

# Chapter Preface

The strategic relationship between Egypt and the United States can be traced to Egypt's emergence from colonial rule under Great Britain and its development as a regional power in the Arab world in the 1950s. Today, the United States views Egypt as a key ally in the Middle East and the most powerful moderate influence in a volatile region.

In 1956 former military leader Gamal Abdel Nasser became president of Egypt. A fiercely nationalistic and popular leader, Nasser clashed with Western governments as a result of his recognition of Communist China, his warm relationship with the Soviet Union, and his support for socialist policies. When the United States and Great Britain abruptly cancelled their offer to help finance the Aswan Dam, a large and expensive public works project on the Nile River, Nasser responded by nationalizing the Suez Canal, a man-made waterway connecting the Mediterranean Sea and the Red Sea. This led to the Suez Crisis, in which Israel, France, and Great Britain launched an attack to gain control of the Suez Canal from Egyptian forces in October of 1956. Under serious diplomatic pressure from the United States, the situation was resolved and forces were withdrawn from the region.

The US role as mediator in the Suez Crisis signaled a turning point in US-Egyptian relations. When Egyptian president Anwar Sadat began to soften on the idea of negotiating peace with Israel in the mid-1970s, the relationship between the United States and Egypt strengthened. The United States perceived Egypt to be a vital partner in the Middle East peace process and viewed Egypt's position in the region to be critical to peace between Israel and its Arab neighbors.

Negotiations between Israel and Egypt in the late 1970s, mediated by US diplomatic officials, resulted in the historic Camp David peace accords. Sadat also implemented economic reforms to modernize the nation's stagnant economy and opened up a multiparty political system.

Under Sadat's successor, Hosni Mubarak, US-Egyptian relations remained warm and based on strategic concerns. Mubarak's government provided vital counterterrorism support after the terrorist attacks of September 11, 2001, on the United States. Friction between the two countries developed, however, when Egypt opposed the war in Iraq and refused to send peacekeeping troops to Afghanistan and Iraq. On the Egyptian side, an intensifying anti-American feeling was voiced by many Egyptians who believed that Americans ignored Mubarak's heavy-handed tactics and domestic abuses.

Leading up to the 2011 revolution that ousted Mubarak from power, the United States urged the Egyptian leader to implement much-needed economic and political reforms and address the reports of widespread human rights violations. During the next few tumultuous years in Egypt's history, which included Mubarak's forced resignation, the democratic election of Mohamed Morsi and his ouster on July 3, 2013, and the election of former military leader Abdel Fattah al-Sisi as president, the United States has continued to underscore its commitment to a democratic Egypt.

US secretary of state John Kerry reaffirmed that commitment in remarks he made after a meeting with Egyptian foreign minister Nabil Fahmy on November 3, 2013. "The United States wants Egypt to succeed and we want to contribute to your success. . . . As I told Minister Fahmy in our meeting this morning, Egypt is a vital partner to America in this region. As the home to a quarter of the Arab world, Egypt plays a crucial role in the political, cultural, and economic leadership of the Middle East and North Africa," stated Kerry.

With the election of Sisi as president of Egypt in 2014, US-Egyptian relations enter a new phase. The following chapter considers what US policy in Egypt should be.

> "Given the depths of our partnership
> with Egypt, our national security inter-
> est in this pivotal part of the world and
> our belief that engagement can support
> a transition back to a democratically
> elected civilian government, we've sus-
> tained our commitment to Egypt and
> its people."

# The United States Will Support Democratic and Economic Reform in Egypt

*Barack Obama*

*Barack Obama is the forty-fourth president of the United States.
In the following viewpoint, he expresses his concern over the
overthrow of the democratically elected Egyptian government in
2013, and he criticizes the military government for its violent
crackdown on dissenters and supporters of former president Mohamed Morsi and the Muslim Brotherhood. President Obama
suggests that although the United States does not believe that
force was the right path to take in this situation, it is time to
look forward, bring about reconciliation with Muslim Brotherhood supporters, and set the country back on a path of demo-*

Barack Obama, "Remarks on Egypt," Whitehouse.gov, August 15, 2013.

*cratic reform. He calls on the interim government to respect the rights of the Egyptian people, begin a national process of reconciliation, and implement economic reforms to spur economic growth. Obama maintains that it is within the interests of the United States to have a peaceful, democratic, and prosperous Egypt.*

As you read, consider the following questions:

1. Back to what does President Obama trace the relationship between the United States and Egypt?

2. According to President Obama, what cycle needs to stop for the sake of the Egyptian people?

3. President Obama says that it is tempting to blame whom for what has gone wrong in Egypt?

I just finished a discussion with my national security team about the situation in Egypt [in August 2013], and I wanted to provide an update about our response to the events of the last several days.

Let me begin by stepping back for a moment. The relationship between the United States and Egypt goes back decades. It's rooted in our respect of Egypt as a nation, an ancient center of civilization and a cornerstone for peace in the Middle East. It's also rooted in our ties to the Egyptian people, forged through a long-standing partnership.

Just over two years ago, America was inspired by the Egyptian people's desire for change, as millions of Egyptians took to the streets to defend their dignity and demand a government that was responsive to their aspirations for political freedom and economic opportunity. And we said at the time that change would not come quickly or easily, but we did align ourselves with a set of principles: nonviolence, a respect for universal rights, and a process for political and economic reform. In doing so, we were guided by values but also by interests, because we believe nations are more stable and more successful when they're guided by those principles as well.

## A Growing Concern

And that's why we're so concerned by recent events. We appreciate the complexity of the situation. While [Mohamed] Morsi was elected president in a democratic election, his government was not inclusive and did not respect the views of all Egyptians.

We know that many Egyptians, millions of Egyptians, perhaps even a majority of Egyptians were calling for a change in course. And while we do not believe that force is the way to resolve political differences, after the military's intervention several weeks ago, there remained a chance for reconciliation and an opportunity to pursue a democratic path. Instead, we've seen a more dangerous path taken, through arbitrary arrests, a broad crackdown on Mr. Morsi's associations and supporters and now, tragically, violence that's taken the lives of hundreds of people and wounded thousands more.

The United States strongly condemns the steps that have been taken by Egypt's interim government and security forces. We deplore violence against civilians. We support universal rights essential to human dignity, including the right to peaceful protest. We oppose the pursuit of martial law, which denies those rights to citizens under the principle that security trumps individual freedom or that might makes right. And today the United States extends its condolences to the families or those who were killed and those who were wounded.

Given the depths of our partnership with Egypt, our national security interest in this pivotal part of the world and our belief that engagement can support a transition back to a democratically elected civilian government, we've sustained our commitment to Egypt and its people. But while we want

## President Barack Obama

Barack Obama is the forty-fourth president of the United States and the first African American to hold that office. A Democratic senator from Illinois at the time of his election in November of 2008, Obama prevailed after a grueling primary season against his chief Democratic rival, Senator Hillary Clinton, and a hard-fought presidential campaign against the Republican candidate, Senator John McCain. Obama electrified voters during campaign appearances with a unifying message of hope and an ambitious agenda of change that included ending the war in Iraq and extending affordable health care to all Americans. In his inaugural address on January 20, 2009, he proclaimed: "On this day, we gather because we have chosen hope over fear, unity of purpose over conflict and discord. . . . The time has come to reaffirm our enduring spirit; to choose our better history; to carry forward that precious gift, that noble idea, passed on from generation to generation: the God-given promise that all are equal, all are free, and all deserve a chance to pursue their full measure of happiness." . . . President Obama was reelected on November 6, 2012.

*"Barack Obama,"*
Contemporary Black Biography, *vol. 74,*
*Biography in Context. Detroit, MI: Gale, 2013.*

to sustain our relationship with Egypt, our traditional cooperation cannot continue as usual when civilians are being killed in the streets and rights are being rolled back.

As a result, this morning we notified the Egyptian government that we are canceling our biannual joint military exercise, which was scheduled for next month.

## Moving Forward

Going forward, I've asked my national security team to assess the implications of the actions taken by the interim government and further steps that we may take as necessary with respect to the U.S.-Egyptian relationship.

Let me say that the Egyptian people deserve better than what we've seen over the last several days. And to the Egyptian people, let me say the cycle of violence and escalation needs to stop. We call on the Egyptian authorities to respect the universal rights of the people. We call on those who are protesting to do so peacefully and condemn the attacks that we've seen by protesters, including on churches. We believe that the state of emergency should be lifted, that a process of national reconciliation should begin, that all parties need to have a voice in Egypt's future, that the rights of women and religious minorities should be respected and that commitments must be kept to pursue transparent reforms to the constitution and democratic elections of a parliament and a president.

And pursuing that path will help Egypt meet the democratic aspirations of its people while attracting the investment, tourism and international support that can help it deliver opportunities to its citizens. Violence, on the other hand, will only feed the cycle of polarization that isolates Egyptians from one another and from the world and that continues to hamper the opportunity for Egypt to get back on the path of economic growth.

Let me make one final point. America cannot determine the future of Egypt. That's a task for the Egyptian people. We don't take sides with any particular party or political figure. I know it's tempting inside of Egypt to blame the United States or the West or some other outside actor for what's gone wrong.

## American Interests

We've been blamed by supporters of Morsi; we've been blamed by the other side as if we are supporters of Morsi. That kind of approach will do nothing to help Egyptians achieve the future that they deserve. We want Egypt to succeed. We want a peaceful, democratic, prosperous Egypt. That's our interest. But to achieve that, the Egyptians are going to have to do the work.

We recognize that change takes time and that a process like this is never guaranteed. There are examples in recent history of countries that are transitioned out of a military government towards a democratic government. And it did not always go in a straight line and the process was not always smooth.

There are going to be false starts. There will be difficult days. America's democratic journey took us through some mighty struggles to perfect our union. From Asia to the Americas, we know that democratic transitions are measured not in months or even years but sometimes in generations.

So in the spirit of mutual interest and mutual respect, I want to be clear that America wants to partner in the Egyptian people's pursuit of a better future. And we are guided by our national interest in this long-standing relationship. But our partnership must also advance the principles that we believe in and that so many Egyptians have sacrificed for these last several years, no matter what party or faction they belong to.

So America will work with all those in Egypt and around the world who support a future of stability that rests on a foundation of justice and peace and dignity. Thank you very much.

*"Egyptian politics and the country's re-cent instability compromise the efficacy of outside assistance."*

# The United States Should Realize the Limitations of Its Influence in Egypt

## Steven A. Cook

*Steven A. Cook is a blogger, author, journalist, and senior fellow for Middle Eastern studies at the Council on Foreign Relations. In the following viewpoint, he underscores the need for the United States to advocate principles of personal freedom, nonvio-lence, governmental transparency, and social justice in Egypt, but he argues that there are limits to what the United States can do in the current situation. Cook outlines two prevailing theories of how democracies emerge: in the first, the right prerequisites exist and lead to a democratic society; in the second, political elites determine that it is within their self-interest to push demo-cratic ideals. The United States has limited influence in either of these scenarios to impel the development of a democratic Egyp-tian state. Cook predicts that Egypt's political order will be the*

*result of a battle between the military, intelligence services, po-
lice, and elements of the opposition in the nation's bureaucratic
order.*

As you read, consider the following questions:

1. What *Foreign Policy* columnist does Cook identify as the
   one who skewered the White House for failing to talk
   tough to the Egyptian military about its undemocratic
   approach?

2. What country does the author cite as the most influential in the global economy?

3. What example does Cook cite as one in which an outside power had a decisive influence on the direction of
   politics in another country?

Over the last week or so [in November 2013], there have
been more than a few stinging indictments of U.S.–
Middle East policy. Whether it is Iran's nuclear program, the
civil war in Syria, or Secretary of State John Kerry's effort to
push Israeli-Palestinian peace talks, the [Barack] Obama administration is near universally derided as both timorous and
out-classed in the face of formidable adversaries. It's been an
impressive pile-on, even if some of this commentary is actually more about politics than analysis. Among the various op-
eds, columns, and articles, two caught my attention. On November 8 in his regular column for *Foreign Policy*, James Traub
skewered the White House for failing to talk tough to the
Egyptian military about its blatantly undemocratic approach
to post–[Mohamed] Morsi Egypt. A few days later, the *Washington Post's* deputy editorial page editor, Jackson Diehl, published a stem-winder of a column that ripped Kerry on every
important issue in the Middle East, including the secretary's
apparent willingness to accommodate what is shaping up to
be Egypt's nondemocratic transition.

Traub and Diehl are serious and accomplished observers of American foreign policy and their contributions to the recent foreign policy debate are not politically motivated. Yet the assumption underlying their articles that the United States can be an anchor of reform in Egypt—a view that is shared among a diverse and influential subset of the American foreign policy elite—is suspect. Before I am accused of being a troglodyte, let me be clear: Democracy in Egypt would be a very good development, providing Egyptians with the representative government they have long sought. I have also written that Washington's approach to Egypt over the last three years should have emphasized principles like personal freedom, nonviolence, transparency, and equal application of the law. That said, it strikes me as odd—given the available evidence—that analysts believe democracy promotion, whether in the form of actual programs designed to encourage more open and just societies or rhetorical support for progressive change, would make an appreciable difference in Egypt.

## The Limits of U.S. Influence

My skepticism is a function of the fact that for Egyptians, the stakes are so high in their struggle to define new political and social institutions, there is very little that external powers can say or do to influence the way in which sons and daughters of the Nile calculate what is best for Egypt. It is also based on my sneaking suspicion that in the end, the people who were central to making the January 25 and June 30 uprisings happen will not determine the trajectory of Egyptian politics. Instead, the contours of Egypt's new political order will likely be determined in a war of position among the military, intelligence services, police, and the counterrevolutionaries embedded in the bureaucracy. Needless to say, this is not a propitious environment in which America's limited resources can make much of a difference.

There is a larger issue than the particulars of the current Egyptian political environment, however. There have been reams and reams written about how and why democracies emerge. Within the academic literature, there are essentially two different schools of thought. The first emphasizes "prerequisites" for democracy—for example, the emergence of a middle class; a certain level of economic development; national unity; and political culture. The second focuses on the calculations of elites. This so-called rationalist approach posits that transitions to democracy occur when political circumstances alter the incentives and constraints of a prevailing elite seeking to survive. This is the way that leaders who have no particular commitment to democratic ideals become democrats. I am simplifying, of course, and the work on transition to democracy is rich, but much of it is built on these two schools of thought.

## The Role the United States Can Play in Egypt

Now, back to Egypt. If we take the two primary conceptions of how democracy emerges seriously, what can the United States reasonably do? Among prerequisites for democracy, it seems that, in the abstract, the United States can actually do something about wealth. The United States still occupies the most influential position in the global economy, calls the shots at international financial institutions like the IMF [International Monetary Fund], and holds significant economic influence in Europe and Asia. Yet for all that power and prestige, America's global economic influence seems to be eroding due to the rise of others and Washington's dysfunctional politics. The combination of the two makes it difficult to marshal support both at home and abroad to help Egypt economically. Yet Washington is only half the problem. Egyptian politics and the country's recent instability compromise the efficacy of outside assistance.

## U.S.-Egyptian Relations

The United States established diplomatic relations with Egypt in 1922, following its independence from protectorate status under the United Kingdom. The United States and Egypt share a relationship based on mutual interest in Middle East peace and stability, revitalizing the Egyptian economy and strengthening trade relations, and promoting regional security. Egypt has been a key U.S. partner in ensuring regional stability and on a wide range of common security issues, including Middle East peace and countering terrorism.

Egypt's historic transition to democracy, launched in early 2011, will have a profound impact on the political future, not only of Egypt, but also the Middle East and North Africa (MENA) region at large. Supporting a successful transition to democracy and economic stability in Egypt, one that protects the basic rights of its citizens and fulfills the aspirations of the Egyptian people, will continue to be a core objective of U.S. policy toward Egypt. A prosperous and democratic Egypt, buoyed by economic growth and a strong private sector, can be an anchor of stability for the MENA region.

*"U.S. Relations with Egypt,"*
*US Department of State, May 20, 2014.*

If the United States has little capacity to encourage the development of what some believe to be prerequisites for democracy, its ability to shape the calculations of its leaders is also quite limited. What incentive can Washington offer that will alter the interests and constraints of Egypt's leaders? It's unlikely that even if the United States had the resources and political will to offer, for example, billions of aid in exchange for democratic change that Major General Abdel Fattah al-Sisi would respond positively. As noted above, under circumstances in which Egyptians believe they are in an existential struggle for the soul of the country, outsiders—any outsiders—will have very little influence to compel the leaders to do something they would not otherwise do. For all the money that the Saudis, Emiratis, and Kuwaitis are providing, they are merely helping to enable what the Egyptian armed forces would have done anyway.

There may be other examples, but I can only think of one instance in which an outside power had a decisive influence on the direction of politics in a country: the EU [European Union] and Turkey. The prospect of membership in the European Union altered the incentives of Turkish Islamists and placed constraints on Turkey's senior military officers in ways that made the wide-ranging democratic reforms (which have turned out to be reversible) of 2003–2004 possible. The Turkish relationship with the EU is unique, however. As long as there seemed to be a credible chance for Turks to become members of Europe, Brussels had a dynamic effect on Turkish politics. The United States, in contrast, is not going to offer Egypt membership in its own exclusive club.

In a world that some imagine, the United States has the moral, political, and financial authority to promote democratic change in countries thousands of miles away from its shores. I suppose this is the burden of having made "the world safe for democracy"—even though we really did not—and facing down fascism as well as communism. Given this history, I can understand why it is difficult to accept the fact that the traditional tools of American diplomacy do not actually matter much in the struggle for Egypt. We should get used to it.

> *"Because our resources are not unlimited, we have to focus our political time and attention, as well as our more tangible assets and capabilities, where they can do the most good."*

# As Egypt Erupts, U.S. Dithers

*John Bolton*

*John Bolton is a political columnist, television commentator, senior fellow at the American Enterprise Institute (AEI), and former US ambassador to the United Nations. In the following viewpoint, he argues that the United States must define its priorities in Egypt and focus on advancing those interests in practical ways. Bolton outlines what he believes to be the most vital US interests: first, Egypt's continued adherence to the Camp David peace agreement; and second, to protect the Suez Canal. Bolton says that the Muslim Brotherhood should not be allowed to participate in Egyptian politics because the group rejects the Camp David peace accords and would threaten the fragile peace established between Egypt and Israel. Bolton also suggests that the United States continue to give economic aid to the Egyptian military.*

As you read, consider the following questions:

1. According to Bolton, what Egyptian leader was courageous enough to negotiate directly with Israel to establish the 1979 Camp David peace treaty?

2. What Islamist group does Bolton identity as the one
responsible for the assassination of Egyptian leader Anwar Sadat?

3. In what two historical events was passage to the Suez
Canal blocked, according to the author?

Egypt's security forces have now moved decisively to eliminate Muslim Brotherhood protest camps in Cairo, producing the bloodshed foretold by daily confrontations between
the Brotherhood's supporters and opponents. Six weeks after
the ouster of President [Mohamed] Morsi, Egypt remains
deeply and violently divided—and American policy is con-
fused and irresolute.

While confusion and irresolution are nothing new to the
Obama administration, this is not the place to dither or make
strategic mistakes. We must define precisely what U.S. priorities are in light of Egypt's strategic significance, and given the
potential for protracted hostilities there between armed com-
batants.

By identifying our interests, we can concentrate our ener-
gies and resources on advancing them in practical ways, avoid-
ing an essentially academic debate over issues we can't significantly influence. Because our resources are not unlimited, we
have to focus our political time and attention, as well as our
more tangible assets and capabilities, where they can do the
most good.

First, Egypt's continued adherence to the 1979 Camp David
peace agreements with Israel is essential. Anwar Sadat's courageous decision to negotiate directly with Israel was critical not
only to establishing this foundation of America's overall

© Jehad Awrtani/Cartoonstock.com.

Middle East policy, but also evidenced Egypt's momentous shift, after the death of longtime dictator Gamal Abdel Nasser, away from the Soviet Union. Sadat's sea change in allegiance provided an opening the U.S. used to undermine Moscow's extensive regional influence, and was an early sign that the Cold War was entirely winnable.

In 1981, the Muslim Brotherhood assassinated Sadat for his troubles, reflecting that then, as now, the Brotherhood has only contempt for Egyptian leaders who seek peace with Israel. If Morsi had enjoyed only a slightly longer tenure in office, he would likely have abrogated Camp David entirely. The treaty's demise would have even further reduced U.S. influence throughout the Middle East, renewed opportunities for anti-American, anti-Israeli radicals and increased threats to friendly Arab regimes prepared to live with Egyptian (and Jordanian) peace treaties with Israel. Make no mistake, if Washington takes Camp David for granted, it will disappear, and quickly.

Second, the economically vital Suez Canal runs through Egypt. If passage is blocked, as it was in the 1956 Suez Canal crisis, or for years after the 1967 Six-Day War, Europe and America will suffer, and so will Egypt. Already, 2 1/2 years of domestic instability have made the Sinai Peninsula a haven for terrorists and devastated Egypt's economy, with both foreign investment and tourism revenues plummeting.

Until political stability is restored, the nation's gross domestic product will continue eroding, impoverishing the entire society and further straining already weakened social cohesion.

What Washington needs to do is clear. U.S. policy should be to support only Egyptian leaders unambiguously committed to Camp David, both to its terms and to its broader regional significance. And we must assist those who place highest priority on repairing Egypt's badly weakened economy and securing its international economic obligations, particularly safe transit through the Suez Canal.

Both Egypt's military and its "pro-democracy" elements support Camp David, while the Brotherhood does not. There is, accordingly, no reason to advocate including the Brotherhood into a "coalition" form of government or, frankly, to welcome them into the political process at all.

After World War II, we struggled without qualms to keep Communist parties from prevailing in Western European elections; there is every reason to take the same role here.

In particular, that means keeping aid flowing to Egypt's military, which since 1979 has brought its leadership close to Washington. We should fix whatever U.S. statutory problem exists, and encourage Europe and friendly Arab states to follow our lead. We should also leave our Egyptian friends flexibility in their internal political debates.

This does not mean granting them a completely blank check. It does mean rejecting the Obama approach of essentially supporting the Muslim Brotherhood, which is as much an armed militia as a political party, and condemning the interim government.

We all have admirable philosophical ideals about perfect democracy, but these must now be for university debates, not judging the punctilio of daily Egyptian politics.

What is happening in Egypt now is not pretty. We should take care that our efforts to improve things don't make them worse, disrupting our larger regional and worldwide interests.

*"Commitment to the democratic process has been undermined by the continued reluctance and equivocation of the US and others to call a spade a spade."*

# The United States Must Clearly Repudiate the Egyptian Military Coup

*John Esposito*

*John Esposito is an author and professor at Georgetown University. In the following viewpoint, he suggests that the United States needs to stop living in denial and acknowledge that the overthrow of the democratically elected government of Mohamed Morsi was a military coup. If the United States fails to do this, he argues, it will engender a rise in anti-American sentiment that may well become a major security threat in the near future. He notes that the United States has a long and sordid history of supporting military coups in foreign countries when such coups support US interests. He contends that if the United States truly supports a democratic and independent Egypt, it must clearly repudiate the military coup and the widespread repression of Muslim Brotherhood supporters to remain a credible influence in the region.*

As you read, consider the following questions:

1. According to the author, how many Muslim Brotherhood supporters were killed or injured in a recent nonviolent demonstration protesting the 2013 military coup?

2. What two countries does Esposito identify as quick to promise billions of dollars in aid after the democratically elected government of Mohamed Morsi was deposed by the military junta?

3. How many Algerians were killed in the civil war that lasted from 1991 to 2002?

Living in denial never ends well, and failure to recognise Egypt's military coup will prove counterproductive for both Egyptians and Western policy makers.

## A Crucial Test for the US

The US is hard-pressed to recognise the importance of calling [Mohamed] Morsi's removal and the appointment of leadership by the military for what it is, a coup. If mishandled by the military and interim government, Egypt could be set back for at least another generation, adding to modern Egypt's 60-year history of authoritarian rule. At the same time, it will generate anti-Western sentiment that may well become a significant security threat.

The US and Europe will be judged against their espoused principles and values, their commitment to the promotion of democracy and human rights. Thus far they are failing the test, much as they did for decades when they supported authoritarian regimes in Egypt, Tunisia, Latin America, and elsewhere. The US and EU [European Union] need to act now to counter the hardening perception, based on leaks and credible reporting, that the US knew about and—both through its actions and calculated inaction—supported the military coup.

## Protecting the Democratic Process

Commitment to the democratic process has been undermined by the continued reluctance and equivocation of the US and others to call a spade a spade. The overthrow of a democratically elected government and its replacement by military-appointed officials is a coup. At the heart of democracy is a commitment to the democratic process and acceptance of the notion of a loyal opposition. Political leaders are elected to office and turned out of office through recourse to the ballot box. The opposition can oppose, even despise, incumbents and employ every legal means to turn them out of office but they remain loyal to the nation and the democratic process or the entire system has no basis of legitimacy. As Mohamed Adel Ismail, a 26-year-old Egyptian social worker put it: "He [Morsi] made some catastrophic mistakes, that must be said, but my understanding of democracy is you allow him to rule and fail and then vote him out."

Despite the "interim government," led by former [Hosni] Mubarak–appointed officials, making promises of political inclusion and a more democratic process, Morsi has been held incommunicado amidst talk of future charges of sedition or other crimes. The [Muslim] Brotherhood [MB] has been subjected to widespread arrests and detention and denounced as terrorists as the military guns down and beats nonviolent demonstrators—most recently killing some 51 people and injuring more than 400. The military's purpose is transparent and in line with the modus operandi of Mubarak for decades: use brute force to intimidate, repress, and provoke the opposition to violence and then say, "Look, I told you they were wolves in sheep's clothing".

The perception of existential threat that the Brotherhood now feels must be alleviated. Immediate steps by the US and EU in this direction would include demanding to meet with President Morsi immediately, and demand his immediate release as well as that of all political prisoners and detained family members. In addition, the call for a national dialogue that includes the FJP [the Freedom and Justice Party], military representatives, and other political parties in order to identify a path forward that is acceptable to all.

## A Fully Inclusive System

The US and EU must also call for an independent investigation into the attacks on demonstrators and a process by which any parties that used excessive force will be held accountable. It is important the US and EU stress that any future democratic process must allow for the full inclusion of any and all political parties that have participated in post-Mubarak elections, calling for the setting and strict adherence to a date in the near future for elections in which all parties (including the FJP) are able to participate.

To have the above goals taken seriously by the military-backed government, the US and EU must use their only effective bargaining chip for leverage: the cutoff of military aid in accordance with law, and the withholding of recognition of an interim government until the above steps are taken. At the same time, they should carefully monitor the treatment of Morsi, MB and FJP members, and their supporters and denounce in unequivocal terms the use of weapons against unarmed protestors. This would send a clear message to those currently in power and to the Arab world.

## A Step Backward

The Arab uprisings signaled a desire for a new way forward, an overthrow of the established order in many Arab countries of authoritarian governments, and a struggle to establish a new kind of democracy. A military-backed coup is clearly a return to the past. Egypt's first democratically elected president was bound to make mistakes, due to the "democratic deficit" in both systems and culture as a result of decades of authoritarian rule.

Indeed, Morsi and the Brotherhood leadership made many mistakes. They proved ill-equipped to make the transition from a movement organised and geared to survival under threat of siege to an inclusive sufficiently representative (politically and religiously) government. But they also did not control the vast majority of the government bureaucracy, including the military, intelligence, judiciary, interior ministry and police forces, which were—and remain still—remnants of the Mubarak regime. This constitutes a deep state bent on bringing down the Morsi government and likely any other that threatens their stranglehold on power and privileges behind the scenes. The international community: US, IMF [International Monetary Fund], a variety of European countries, Saudi Arabia, and the UAE [United Arab Emirates], were all lukewarm at best and aggressively obstructionist at worst in assisting the Morsi government to address the daunting challenge of an inherited failed economy and high unemployment. Yet within days after the coup, Saudi and the UAE were quick to promise billions of dollars in aid.

The message the [Barack] Obama administration is sending, whether intended or not, is that there is a double standard, much as there was in the decades of US support for authoritarian regimes of the past. Now, in emerging democracies, the rules of the game do not apply to a democratically elected Islamic government. This is reflected in the Obama administration's equivocation and, in effect, denial that the removal of Morsi was a coup just as it was reflected when the George W. Bush administration equivocated about calling waterboarding torture or the rendition programme a violation of human rights and international law. And before him, his father George H.W. Bush's administration's agreement to the Algerian military's takeover in the face of the Islamic Salvation Front's electoral victory, resulting in a "dirty war" that left more than 150,000 Algerians dead in a population of about 25 million.

Long-term Western nations' interests in Egypt, and the wider region, are best served through representative governments elected through a democratic process, rule of law, and independent institutions.

> "If the aid remains frozen, the United
> States risks losing the strategic benefits
> derived from its military-assistance re-
> lationship with Cairo."

# The United States Should Resume Military Aid to Egypt

*Eric Trager*

*Eric Trager is a fellow at the Washington Institute for Near East Policy. In the following viewpoint, he articulates the strategic importance of military aid to Egypt, urging US secretary of state John Kerry and other diplomatic officials to make the case to Congress members that they should not cut off aid to the country at this crucial time. The growing movement to cut off aid to Egypt stems from alarm over the escalating violence and oppression perpetrated by the military government. The concern of American officials at these reports is understandable, Trager states, but the Egyptian government is too fractured for withholding aid to influence the regime's behavior. Instead, Trager argues, it will only serve to damage US-Egyptian relations in the long run.*

As you read, consider the following questions:

1. According to Trager, how much did the Obama administration request in military assistance to Egypt in April 2014?

2. According to Michele Dunne and Scott Williamson of the Carnegie Endowment for International Peace, how many civilians were killed in Egypt between July 2013 and January 2014?

3. What region of Egypt does the author identify as the site of conflict between Egyptian security forces and Islamic jihadists since September 2013?

Given the important strategic interests at stake and the unlikelihood of changing Cairo's short-term behavior, Secretary [John] Kerry should be prepared to use all available options to keep the aid flowing.

The [Barack] Obama administration's attempt to resume military aid to Egypt faces critical opposition in Congress. On Tuesday [in April 2014], Sen. Patrick Leahy (D-VT), who chairs the subcommittee that oversees foreign aid, placed a hold on the administration's April 25 request for $650 million in military assistance to Egypt, stating that the committee needed to see "convincing evidence the government is committed to the rule of law." A bipartisan group of senators backed his efforts.

While concerns regarding Egypt's repressive trajectory are well placed, the administration should urgently press its case. If the aid remains frozen, the United States risks losing the strategic benefits derived from its military-assistance relationship with Cairo. Withholding aid is also unlikely to influence Egypt's domestic political behavior in the short run, and will undermine Washington's ability to influence Cairo in the future, when such pressure might have a greater impact.

## The Role of U.S. Aid to Egypt

U.S. assistance to Egypt has long played a central role in Egypt's economic and military development, and in furthering the strategic partnership. With Egypt embarking on a transition to democracy, U.S. support can bolster Egypt's nascent democratic system and achieve inclusive economic growth. U.S. assistance supports Egyptian efforts to protect civil liberties and human rights; introduce transparency and accountability in government; foster economic growth and democratic institutions; and develop a robust, independent civil society.

*"U.S. Relations with Egypt,"*
*US Department of State, May 20, 2014.*

## Growing Repression and Violence in Egypt

The renewed calls to withhold aid came in the wake of two Egyptian court decisions announced on Monday, in which 720 alleged Muslim Brotherhood members were sentenced to death for the killing of two police officers. The calls also reflect mounting dismay at Cairo's unrelenting repression since the military responded to mass protests by removing President [Mohamed] Morsi last summer. According to Michele Dunne and Scott Williamson of the Carnegie Endowment for International Peace, over 2,500 civilians were killed between July 2013 and January 2014, in addition to 17,000 wounded and 18,000 detained. The crackdown has also broadened beyond the disempowered Brotherhood: Activists campaigning against the January constitutional referendum were recently sentenced to three years in prison, and the courts have outlawed the revolutionary April 6 Youth Movement, which backed Morsi's ouster.

Again, while concerns about these developments are justified, the call to withhold military aid misunderstands both the nature of the current Egyptian government and Washington's capacity for influencing it. Unlike the Hosni Mubarak era, when power was largely centralized in the dictator's hands, the new government is severely fractured, with competing power centers—particularly the military, police, and judiciary—acting independently. Withholding aid occasionally compelled Mubarak to change his behavior, but that tool will not work as effectively now because the state's fractured nature means that each institution controls little outside of its own domain. For example, the military now has little influence over the judiciary and therefore cannot undo the hundreds of death sentences that the courts have issued recently, most of which will likely be commuted on appeal. Indeed, top-ranking generals privately say that they not only oppose these sentences, but are profoundly embarrassed by them.

## Limited Impact

Under these circumstances, U.S. military aid can reliably impact only one thing: the Egyptian military's external behavior. To be sure, the military has its own reasons for maintaining strategic cooperation with Washington—apart from the fact that a majority of Egypt's arsenal consists of American-made weapons, many of its officers have trained in U.S. military academies, and policies such as maintaining the peace treaty with Israel and fighting terrorism in the Sinai are in its own interest. Even so, withholding aid could still jeopardize Washington's ability to ensure Egypt's longer-term cooperation. For one thing, Russia is trying to expand its influence in the Middle East by selling weapons to Cairo, and various Persian Gulf states—which have sent billions in aid to keep the current Egyptian government afloat—are strongly supporting Moscow's efforts. Moreover, after years of refusing to do so, the Egyptian military has been actively fighting Sinai-based jihadists since September, so withholding aid now would send a very confusing message about Washington's strategic priorities. The United States also stands to lose other strategic benefits if the aid is withheld, including overflight rights and preferred access to the Suez Canal.

Finally, the deeply fractured government currently running Egypt might become more consolidated a few months from now, when former defense minister Abdel Fattah al-Sisi will likely be president. Under those circumstances, using military aid to encourage a more progressive political atmosphere might make a difference. But if Washington withholds aid now, it will lose the leverage needed to influence Cairo down the road, in addition to having no significant effect on Egypt's troubling trajectory in the short term. For all of these reasons, Secretary of State John Kerry should be prepared to use what options are available to him to ensure the aid continues.

> *"Is it even possible for the US to follow the European Union's moral lead and suspend the export of all equipment that could be used by the Egyptian military regime in its ongoing campaign of repression?"*

# The United States Should Not Resume Military Aid to Egypt

*Sarah Marusek*

*Sarah Marusek is a journalist and political activist. In the following viewpoint, she examines the controversy over the United States resuming military aid to Egypt in light of the military regime's widespread human rights violations and political oppression. Marusek reports that the United States is reluctant to cut off military aid to Egypt for a number of reasons. One is that the US government is being pressured by Israel to resume military aid out of concern that a suspension of aid will threaten the fragile peace accord between Israel and Egypt. Another is that Egypt has run up a $4 billion debt buying American weapons and military equipment, and cutting off aid means that the US weapons industry will take a huge hit. Marusek contends* *that it is Egypt that holds the upper hand in its relations with the United States because both parties recognize Egypt's vital strategic significance to the West.*

As you read, consider the following questions:

1. According to Marusek, on what day was the Muslim Brotherhood designated a terrorist organization?

2. How much does the United States give to Egypt in military aid every year since the mid-1980s, according to the author?

3. According to Al Jazeera America, how much military equipment was delivered to Egypt after the US government suspended some military assistance to the country in October 2013?

Ever since the 3 July [2013] military coup that ousted Egypt's first democratically elected government, the world has stood back to witness the Egyptian authorities' brazen attempt to cleanse an entire community from Egypt's population.

As an American citizen I have to ask: How many Egyptians need to be killed, injured, arrested and tortured, and how many families torn apart and destroyed, before the US will take decisive action against Egypt's post-coup military regime?

And I am not the only American asking this question.

On Friday [in January 2014], the *Los Angeles Times* newspaper published an editorial under the headline "Stop coddling Egypt's military". The editors argue that: "It's increasingly evident that the military rulers of Egypt are determined to intimidate and silence their political opponents, whether they are members of the Muslim Brotherhood or secular Egyptians who believe the generals are betraying the spirit of the

'Arab Spring.' Yet the Obama administration continues to entertain the pious hope that Egypt is on the road to an inclusive democracy."

The editors criticise the US response to the continued crackdown as being "polite to the point of pusillanimity", and conclude that, "Clearly the current policy of trying not to offend [Egypt's military] isn't working."

One week earlier, the *Washington Post* newspaper published a similar editorial, in which the editors denounce the Egyptian authorities' criminalisation of the Muslim Brotherhood. The movement was designated a terrorist organisation on 25 December [2013].

The *Post*'s editors lament how "Egypt has abandoned the path to democracy", calling this a "tragedy" and asserting that: "The time has come for stronger US protests and action. To remain timid in the face of repression will invite only more."

So why is the [Barack] Obama administration not acting? After all, the US is supposedly a global superpower, and we have spent billions of dollars buying Egypt's friendship.

Well, if we take a closer look at the two countries' relations, we see that Egypt has never really been a client state of the US, and in fact the relationship is quite the reverse.

## Military Aid and "Peace"

In February 2012, when Egypt's military-led government under SCAF [Supreme Council of the Armed Forces] indicted 16 Americans working for nongovernmental organisations [NGO] in Egypt on charges of receiving foreign funds to foment unrest, US officials were quick to decry the move, and threatened a halt to American military aid to Egypt. In fact, 40 senators sent a strongly worded letter of warning directly to the former head of Egypt's military, Field Marshal Mohamed Hussein Tantawi. Senator Patrick Leahy, the chairman of the Senate Appropriations Committee's subcommittee, warned the Egyptian military that, "the days of blank checks are over."

And yet the following week, the rhetoric coming out of Washington was remarkably softened. According to the *Atlantic* magazine, officials had initially been so caught up in their outrage over the charges against Americans, including the son of the US secretary of transportation, that they did not think about how cutting Egypt's military aid would have implications for their best friend in the Middle East, Israel.

Egypt is currently the fifth-largest recipient of US aid in the world, and cumulatively second only to Israel. Foreign aid to Egypt was negligible until the mid-1970s and only ballooned after Egypt signed the Camp David Accords with Israel in 1978. Since the mid-1980s, Egypt has received annually about $1.3 billion in military aid, while Israel received $1.8 billion until the year 2000, after which military aid to Israel fluctuated between $2 to $3.1 billion.

According to the Washington Institute [for Near East Policy], military aid to Egypt was initially tied to US aid levels to Israel, which is why the figures remained proportional up until 2000, when the launch of the second Palestinian intifada altered the equation. Two other factors also contributed to the shift. The first is that by the turn of the millennium, Egypt was no longer isolated in the region as a result of its neighbourly relations with Israel. The second is that by then, the US had phased out its economic aid to Israel, allocating part of it instead for military use.

## Is It Aid or Blackmail?

Still, continued US aid to Egypt remains an unwritten condition of the Camp David Accords, and since the January 2011 revolution in Egypt, the Israel lobby has repeatedly voiced its concern that if the aid were to dry up, then the peace treaty would be in jeopardy.

So it is not surprising that despite being subject to the harshly worded threats, Egypt continued to prosecute the American NGO workers, a political slap in Washington's face, all the while receiving US military aid. All 16 Americans, along with 27 of their Egyptian peers, were eventually convicted and sentenced in absentia in June 2013.

This case is interesting for two reasons. One is that it highlights how US aid to Egypt is meant first and foremost to please and protect Israel. The second is that the Egyptian military regime knows this, and thus acts with impunity. The case against the 16 American NGO workers illustrates that. But so does the history of US economic aid to Egypt.

The US has always employed its foreign aid as a political tool, and its economic assistance is handled by the US Agency for International Development (USAID). Both during the Cold War and in the neoliberal era, USAID projects have come with conditions strongly favouring free markets and privatisation. But interestingly, in the case of Egypt, scholar Bessma Momani argues that: "the Egyptian government perceived the aid programme as an entitlement for signing the Camp David Accords, where equality of treatment between Egypt and Israel was supposedly guaranteed. In consequence, USAID found that the aid at its disposal did not give the organisation any real influence to induce Egypt to alter its economic policies."

Writing in 1997, scholar Duncan Clarke also noted that Egypt views the American funds as its entitlement for making peace with Israel, thus despite the massive amounts of US aid to Egypt, "The remarkable absence of vigorous, reliable Egyptian advocates of the US is particularly striking." In 1991, the US and its allies even agreed to forgive half the $20.2 billion debt that Egypt owed to them, in thanks for Egypt's support during the Persian Gulf War. Nevertheless, Momani suggests that during this time, the Egyptian government was still not willing to alter its economic policy enough for Washington's liking.

Continually frustrated by Egypt's unwillingness to "reform" its state-driven economy, in 1993 the US decided to privatise its economic aid to Egypt. Momani describes how Cairo and Washington set up a "Presidents' Council" consisting of 15 American and 15 Egyptian corporate representatives to manage private American investment in Egypt as an alternative to official US government aid. Oil executives along with major US multinationals comprised the American team, while companies that had well-established connections with the Egyptian elite and were close to former Egyptian president Hosni Mubarak made up the Egyptian team, which was headed by Mubarak's son Gamal.

In this way Egypt's rulers successfully transformed the US's ideologically driven neoliberal policy into a crony trade relationship that directly profited the Mubarak regime.

## How US Aid to Egypt Works

There are other aspects of the bilateral relationship that also limit Washington's options.

All US military aid to foreign countries is deposited into an account at the Federal Reserve Bank of New York as part of the Foreign Military Financing programme, which is run by a division of the Pentagon called the Defense Security Cooperation Agency (DSCA). Nearly all countries have to spend the funds the US allocates each year, but Egypt is allowed to place orders on credit, which means that Egypt usually has a backlog of orders before the annual aid is even dispersed. The only other country granted this privilege is Israel.

The Washington Institute cites estimates that Egypt currently has about "$4 billion in outstanding contractual commitments to be paid by cash-flow financing". In other words, Egypt has run up a $4 billion debt to satisfy its rapacious appetite for American-made weapons and military equipment, and all at the expense of US taxpayers, whose money is being funneled into the pockets of American weapons manufacturers.

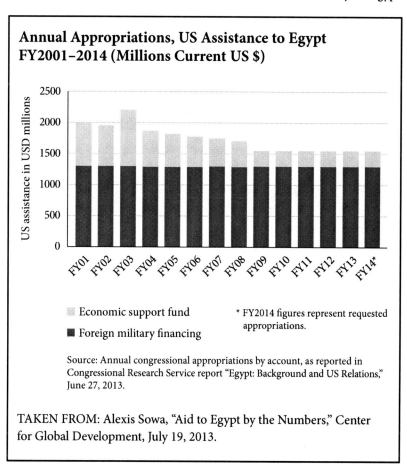

**Annual Appropriations, US Assistance to Egypt FY2001–2014 (Millions Current US $)**

Economic support fund

Foreign military financing

* FY2014 figures represent requested appropriations.

Source: Annual congressional appropriations by account, as reported in Congressional Research Service report "Egypt: Background and US Relations," June 27, 2013.

TAKEN FROM: Alexis Sowa, "Aid to Egypt by the Numbers," Center for Global Development, July 19, 2013.

That's why throughout the recent crackdown, the contracts never stopped coming in. According to the *Politico* web site, the day of the coup the US Army asked for information from contractors interested in building and upgrading F-16 bases in Egypt. And less than one week after the Egyptian security forces massacred and wounded thousands of anti-coup protesters in Rabaa Al-Adawiya and Al-Nahda Squares, "the US Air Force awarded a contract to General Electric to upgrade the Egyptian air force's fighter jets. The deal, worth nearly $14 million, is to extend the lives of 18 engines used on F-16s and other fighters."

The argument goes that cutting military aid to Egypt would mean that US companies would not get paid for the orders they are processing and this would negatively impact the US economy, resulting in job losses. However, maintaining the aid while stopping the delivery of the American-made weapons and military equipment is a possibility.

A report published by *Businessweek* magazine last August noted that, "Once the work is completed and the contractor is paid, it's up to the DSCA to deliver the equipment to Egypt." And according to the report, as of August the agency was not delivering anything.

This included helicopters, fighter aircrafts and tank kits.

The magazine pointed out that: "This wouldn't be the first time the US withheld military equipment it's sold to a foreign country. In 1972, Libyan president Muammar Qaddafi paid $70 million for eight C-130 Hercules aircraft. After political tensions arose and relations between the US and Libya became strained, Washington simply decided not to deliver the planes. To this day the aircraft are still sitting outside Lockheed's plant in Marietta, Ga."

However, according to Al Jazeera America, after the Obama administration announced in early October that it would suspend some military assistance to Egypt, "nearly 2,000 tons of critical US military equipment continued to flow to Egyptian ports." Although there was a delay in the shipment of some fighter jets, other equipment, including several kinds of vehicles used for crowd control, missile systems and spare parts for tanks, helicopters and fighter jets, among other items, continued to depart from eastern US ports to Egypt.

## And Then There Is the "War on Terror"

So if the aid was supposedly halted, what is the catch?

One problem is that the Obama administration has repeatedly vowed to continue its provision of weapons and military equipment to help the Egyptian authorities fight "terrorism" in the Sinai, which shares a border with Israel.

Another is that the shipments mainly contain spare parts. As Al Jazeera America points out, during the 1980s and 1990s, US military aid "led Egypt to phase out its Soviet-made arsenal, replacing most of its military equipment with higher-end US products." Since then, Egypt has amassed an arsenal of American-made weapons and equipment, including thousands of tanks and the fourth-largest fleet of F-16 fighter aircrafts in the world.

"There's no conceivable scenario in which they'd need all those tanks short of an alien invasion," Shana Marshall of the Institute for Middle East Studies at the George Washington University joked to American National Public Radio.

So while Egypt is not in need of more weapons, the existing equipment does get worn out and continues to require a constant supply of spare parts, which the US freely provides. And Marshall also told Al Jazeera America that: "there's a lot of pressure on Congress [from the defence industry] to maintain those production lines in their own districts."

This helps to explain why so many members of Congress, including Eliot Engel of New York, the most senior Democrat on the House Foreign Affairs Committee, expressed "concern" when the Obama administration announced that it was withholding selected aid in October.

That said, some members of Congress did actively lobby to end military aid to Egypt while the country was under the leadership of President [Mohamed] Morsi. The Muslim Brotherhood, after all, always did entertain the possibility of rethinking the Camp David Accords. Of course, these officials failed to realise that during Egypt's short-lived democracy, US military aid went directly to Egypt's military, and not to the civilian government.

## US Public Opinion

In any case, there is public support for an aid freeze. A Pew Research [Center] survey in August found that "51 per cent of Americans believe the US should cut off military aid to Egypt to pressure the government there to end the violence against anti-government protesters." And this number would likely be higher if Americans knew that the dispersal of military aid to Egypt could continue while the deliveries of the weapons are halted, weapons which could then even be sold to other parties for a profit, thus ensuring that American jobs are not lost.

So what is the prognosis for US military aid to Egypt? Is it even possible for the US to follow the European Union's moral lead and suspend the export of all equipment that could be used by the Egyptian military regime in its ongoing campaign of repression?

Although in October President Obama suspended the delivery of some military equipment to Egypt pending the election of a civilian government, Washington still refuses to call the events surrounding 3 July a "coup", a determination that would automatically halt all US military aid to Egypt in accordance with US law. And significantly, right after President Obama announced the suspension, Egypt hired a new Washington lobby firm.

Thus it should be no surprise to hear that before going on winter recess, the Senate Foreign Relations Committee approved a bill on 18 December "that would allow the US to resume its full $1.6 billion aid relationship with Egypt by granting President Obama the power to waive [the federal law on the coup restriction] based on national security," as reported by the Associated Press. Only a few days before the Senate committee passed this bill, three right-wing House Republicans travelled to Cairo to visit General Abdel Fattah al-Sisi: Louie Gohmert of Texas, Steve King of Iowa and Michele Bachmann of Minnesota.

## US Concerns

Considering that for Washington, US national security is mainly defined by two key concerns, Israel and the global war on "terror", and that the three House Republicans have a particular obsession with the Muslim Brotherhood, it is no wonder that Egypt's interim authorities subsequently declared the movement a terrorist organisation.

And yet the new US law also aims to ensure that: "Egypt continues to implement the Egyptian-Israeli peace treaty, is fighting terrorism, is allowing the US Army to transit the territory of Egypt, is supporting a transition to an inclusive civilian government, is respecting and protecting the political and economic freedoms of all Egyptians, is respecting freedom of expression and due process of law, and finally, is abiding by the Nuclear Non-Proliferation Treaty," according to the Egyptian newspaper *Al-Ahram Weekly*.

While none of these conditions are anything particularly new, Hussein Haridy, a former assistant to the Egyptian foreign minister, has declared the bill "a blatant interference in the domestic affairs of Egypt" that must be firmly rejected by the interim authorities.

So despite Egypt's continued human rights abuses and the calls from the American media for Washington to take action, US military aid to Egypt will probably continue to flow. Indeed, considering that in November Egypt negotiated a multibillion-dollar weapons deal with Russia, financed by the petrol dollars of the monarchies in Saudi Arabia and the United Arab Emirates, as well as the historical imbalance of power between the US and Egypt in the latter's favour, it seems more likely that if the aid were ever to be cancelled, then it would be the Egyptian authorities making that decision, not Washington.

# Periodical and Internet Sources Bibliography

*The following articles have been selected to supplement the diverse views presented in this chapter.*

| | |
|---|---|
| Peter Beinart | "The War Over Egypt Is Now Getting Waged in Washington," *Newsweek*, July 10, 2013. |
| Ken Dilanian, Paul Richter, and Laura King | "U.S. Worries Its Aid to Egypt May Be Misdirected," *Los Angeles Times*, April 30, 2014. |
| Dalia Fahmy | "Egypt: Hearts and Minds Betrayed," Al Jazeera, May 9, 2014. |
| Michael Wahid Hanna and Brian Katulis | "Preparing for a Strategic Shift on U.S. Policy Toward Egypt," Center for American Progress, November 30, 2013. |
| Human Rights First | "U.S. Policy Toward Egypt Should Advance Human Rights," April 10, 2014. |
| Human Rights Watch | "Egypt: Failure to Meet US Aid Conditions," April 4, 2014. |
| Ernesto Londoño | "Sen. Leahy Blocks U.S. Aid to Egypt to Protest Nation's 'Appalling Abuse of Justice System,'" *Washington Post*, April 30, 2014. |
| Missy Ryan | "U.S.-Egypt Military Ties Will Depend on Egypt's Actions: U.S. General," Reuters, May 21, 2014. |
| Jim Sciutto and Elise Labott | "U.S. to Cut Some Military Aid to Egypt After Coup, Turmoil," CNN, October 9, 2013. |
| Álvaro Vasconcelos and Michele Dunne | "Getting Egypt Right: Policy Challenges for the EU and the US," *Daily News* (Egypt), May 25, 2014. |
| Jeremy White | "U.S. Military Aid Is Not a Gift, It's a Payment," *Huffington Post*, August 16, 2013. |

# For Further Discussion

## Chapter 1

1. Robert Scheer contends that the military seizure of power in Egypt was a coup. Does Scheer offer sufficient evidence to support his claim? Why, or why not?

2. According to Max Fisher, the events that took place in Egypt in 2013 meet the definition of both a coup and a revolution. How would you define these events? Explain your answer.

3. Hafez Ghanem outlines three possible scenarios for Egypt's future. In your opinion, which of these scenarios are most likely, and why?

## Chapter 2

1. As Sharif Abdel Kouddous points out, thousands of protesters and supporters of Mohamed Morsi and the Muslim Brotherhood have been imprisoned and beaten in Egypt. Based on the facts in the viewpoint, do you believe this activity will continue? Why, or why not?

2. Brian Rohan reports on the growing problem of sexual assault against women in Egypt. How are Egyptian women combating this epidemic? Do you believe this course of action by women will be successful? Explain.

3. Talal Salman examines the corruption in Egypt and the challenges Abdel Fattah al-Sisi faces as president of that country. What are some examples of this corruption and these challenges? Do you think with Sisi as president these challenges and corruption will subside? Explain.

## Chapter 3

1. Salma El Shahed contends that Egypt needs a secular government. Why does she believe this type of government is necessary? Do you agree or disagree with the author? Defend your answer.

2. Asma Afsaruddin argues that political figures use religion to justify political strategies. What evidence does Afsaruddin provide to support this argument? Do you agree with the author? Explain.

3. Jamal Khashoggi asserts that the biggest problem in Egypt is its economy. Do you believe economic reform would improve the political and social strife in Egypt? Explain your answer.

## Chapter 4

1. In his remarks on Egypt, Barack Obama announces that the United States will support political and economic reform in Egypt. In your view, should the United States lend this support? Why, or why not?

2. John Bolton claims that the United States must identify its interests in Egypt and then act to protect them. What reasons does Bolton give for making this argument? Do you agree with Bolton's reasoning? Explain.

3. Eric Trager asserts that the United States should resume military aid to Egypt. Conversely, Sarah Marusek maintains that all US military aid to Egypt should be suspended. With which author do you agree, and why?

# Organizations to Contact

*The editors have compiled the following list of organizations concerned with the issues debated in this book. The descriptions are derived from materials provided by the organizations. All have publications or information available for interested readers. The list was compiled on the date of publication of the present volume; the information provided here may change. Be aware that many organizations take several weeks or longer to respond to inquiries, so allow as much time as possible.*

**Carnegie Endowment for International Peace**
1779 Massachusetts Avenue NW
Washington, DC   20036-2103
(202) 483-7600 • fax: (202) 483-1840
website: www.carnegieendowment.org

The Carnegie Endowment for International Peace is a nonprofit, nonpartisan organization working to advance cooperation between nations and to promote active international engagement by the United States. The organization's website contains a section on Egypt that provides news, links to publications, and other information about the country. Publications available include "Grading Egypt's Roadmap Toward Democracy," "What the United States Wants in Egypt," and "Egypt's Post-Mubarak Predicament."

**Council on Foreign Relations (CFR)**
Harold Pratt House, 58 East Sixty-Eighth Street
New York, NY   10065
(212) 434-9400 • fax: (212) 434-9800
website: www.cfr.org

The Council on Foreign Relations (CFR) is an independent, nonpartisan membership organization, think tank, and publisher dedicated to improving understanding of US foreign policy and international affairs. CFR publishes a bimonthly journal, *Foreign Affairs*, and its website features reports, books, expert interviews, meeting transcripts, videos, crisis guides and timelines, and press releases. A search of CFR's website produces a list of publications related to Egypt, including "Egypt After the Election" and "Egypt's Fateful Verdict."

## Human Rights Watch (HRW)

350 Fifth Avenue, 34th Floor, New York, NY   10118-3299
(212) 290-4700
website: www.hrw.org

Human Rights Watch (HRW) is an independent organization dedicated to defending and protecting human rights worldwide. It seeks to focus international attention on places where human rights are violated, to give voices to the oppressed, and to hold oppressors accountable for their crimes. The HRW website includes numerous reports on human rights in Egypt, including "The Road Ahead: A Human Rights Agenda for Egypt's New Parliament."

## Middle East Institute (MEI)

1761 N Street NW, Washington, DC   20036
(202) 785-1141 • fax: (202) 331-8861
e-mail: information@mei.edu
website: www.mei.edu

The Middle East Institute (MEI) offers unbiased and insightful information on the Middle East to provide a better understanding of the region for policy makers, business leaders, and students. MEI fulfills its mission of increasing knowledge about the Middle East by organizing events and lectures, offering instruction in Middle Eastern languages, and sponsoring research. It publishes the periodical the *Middle East Journal*, and its website offers numerous articles on Egypt, including "Egypt's Election: Beyond the Foregone Conclusion."

## Middle East Media Research Institute (MEMRI)

PO Box 27837, Washington, DC   20038-7837

(202) 955-9070 • fax: (202) 955-9077
e-mail: memri@memri.org
website: www.memri.org

Based in Washington, DC, the Middle East Media Research Institute (MEMRI) is a nonprofit, nonpartisan organization dedicated to monitoring various forms of media in the Middle East. Its aim is to better understand the issues important in the region and to develop an improved understanding of the region's culture and politics. It seeks to provide accurate and relevant information to inform the debate on US policy in the region. MEMRI posts clips of television programs, public speeches, sermons, movies, and Internet video, including "Egyptian Novelist Alaa Al-Aswany: Mubarak's Mentality Still Rules This Country."

### Middle East Policy Council (MEPC)

1730 M Street NW, Suite 512, Washington, DC   20036
(202) 296-6767 • fax: (202) 296-5791
e-mail: info@mepc.org
website: www.mepc.org

The Middle East Policy Council (MEPC) is a nonprofit educational organization that seeks to inform the debate on political, cultural, and economic issues of US interest in the Middle East. MEPC publishes *Middle East Policy*, a quarterly journal that reports on a wide range of subjects related to US foreign policy in the region. A number of articles and commentary by MEPC scholars can be accessed on the organization's website, including "Egypt's Presidential Elections and El Sisi's Road Ahead," "Egypt Must Crush Its Enemies and Ignore Critics," and "Muslim Brotherhood on the Ropes."

### National Council on U.S.-Arab Relations (NCUSAR)

1730 M Street NW, Suite 503, Washington, DC   20036
(202) 293-6466 • fax: (202) 293-7770
website: www.ncusar.org

The National Council on U.S.-Arab Relations (NCUSAR) is a nonprofit organization whose aim is to inform American understanding of the Arab world. It fulfills this goal by offering leadership development programs, educational lectures, and public forums. NCUSAR also holds public educational briefings on Capitol Hill to debate and exchange ideas on US foreign policy in the Middle East and to discuss ways to improve US-Arab relations. The NCUSAR website features a range of articles, policy briefs, videos, newsletters, and audio recordings such as "The Way Forward in Egypt."

## National Endowment for Democracy (NED)

1025 F Street NW, Suite 800, Washington, DC   20004
(202) 378-9700 • fax: (202) 378-9407
e-mail: info@ned.org
website: www.ned.org

The National Endowment for Democracy (NED) is a private, nonprofit organization that works to promote the growth and improvement of democratic institutions worldwide. Within Egypt, NED provides large amounts of money in the form of grants to help strengthen the fight for democracy. NED publishes the quarterly *Journal of Democracy*, and its website provides reports and articles on a variety of topics related to democracy around the world.

## Project on Middle East Democracy (POMED)

1611 Connecticut Avenue NW, Suite 300
Washington, DC   20009
(202) 828-9660
website: www.pomed.org

The Project on Middle East Democracy (POMED) is an independent, nonprofit organization that seeks to advance democracy in the Middle East. POMED organizes conferences and seminars, conducts and disseminates research, and offers analyses, policy papers, and in-depth studies that promote democratic reforms in Middle Eastern countries. These publications, including "U.S. Must Restructure Aid to Egypt," can be accessed on the POMED website.

## United Nations Development Programme (UNDP)

One United Nations Plaza, New York, NY    10017
website: www.undp.org

The United Nations Development Programme (UNDP) works to promote global development and to help connect developing countries with knowledge, experience, and resources to help their citizens build a better life. UNDP has offices and staff in more than 175 countries working to promote democracy, reduce armed conflicts, and mitigate the effects of war and natural disaster. UNDP also coordinates efforts to reach the Millennium Development Goals, a commitment of world leaders to cut world poverty in half by 2015. The UNDP website includes a number of relevant publications, including "UNDP Results: Egypt."

## United States Department of State

2201 C Street NW, Washington, DC    20520
(202) 647-4000
website: www.state.gov

The US Department of State is a federal agency that advises the president on issues of foreign policy. It is responsible for formulating, implementing, and assessing US foreign policy. The State Department's website includes the section Countries & Regions, which provides information about Egypt, including press releases and fact sheets about the country.

## United States Institute of Peace (USIP)

2301 Constitution Avenue NW, Washington, DC    20037
(202) 457-1700
website: www.usip.org

The United States Institute of Peace (USIP) is an independent, nonpartisan institution that is funded by the US Congress to find peaceful methods to mitigate international conflicts. USIP's mission is to "prevent, mitigate and resolve violent conflicts around the world by engaging directly in conflict zones and providing analysis, education and resources to those working for peace." USIP produces a number of publications available on its website, which features its *Olive Branch* blog. The website also offers articles such as "Amid Violence, Egypt's Interim Regime Faces Skeptics on Pledges of Dialogue" and "Prospects for a Democratic Revolution in Egypt."

## World Policy Institute (WPI)
108 West Thirty-Ninth Street, Suite 1000
New York, NY   10018
(212) 481-5005 • fax: (212) 481-5009
e-mail: wpi@worldpolicy.org
website: www.worldpolicy.org

The World Policy Institute (WPI) is among the world's leading think tanks for providing nonpartisan, international policy leadership. The institute works to ensure a stable global market economy open to all; to foster informed global civic participation to create effective governments; and to encourage international cooperation on national and global security issues. WPI's website offers the *World Policy Blog*, which features numerous articles on Egypt, including "Armies of the Arab Spring" and "Egypt's Blurred Lines: Religion and Politics."

# Bibliography of Books

Hussein Ali Agrama — *Questioning Secularism: Islam, Sovereignty, and the Rule of Law in Modern Egypt.* Chicago, IL: University of Chicago Press, 2012.

Holger Albrecht — *Raging Against the Machine: Political Opposition Under Authoritarianism in Egypt.* Syracuse, NY: Syracuse University Press, 2013.

Galal Amin — *Egypt in the Era of Hosni Mubarak.* Cairo, Egypt: American University in Cairo Press, 2011.

Galal Amin — *Whatever Happened to the Egyptian Revolution?* Cairo, Egypt: American University in Cairo Press, 2013.

Saïd Amir Arjomand and Nathan J. Brown, eds. — *The Rule of Law, Islam, and Constitutional Politics in Egypt and Iran.* Albany: State University of New York Press, 2014.

Alaa Al Aswany — *On the State of Egypt: What Made the Revolution Inevitable.* New York: Vintage Books, 2011.

Mohamed El-Bendary — *The Egyptian Revolution: Between Hope and Despair: Mubarak to Morsi.* New York: Algora Publishing, 2013.

Lisa Blaydes — *Elections and Distributive Politics in Mubarak's Egypt.* New York: Cambridge University Press, 2013.

| | |
|---|---|
| Jason Brownlee | *Democracy Prevention: The Politics of the U.S.-Egyptian Alliance*. New York: Cambridge University Press, 2012. |
| Steven A. Cook | *The Struggle for Egypt: From Nasser to Tahrir Square*. New York: Oxford University Press, 2011. |
| Mark Gasiorowski, David E. Long, and Bernard Reich, eds. | *The Government and Politics of the Middle East and North Africa*. Boulder, CO: Westview Press, 2013. |
| James L. Gelvin | *The Arab Uprisings: What Everyone Needs to Know*. New York: Oxford University Press, 2012. |
| Stephen R. Grand | *Understanding Tahrir Square: What Transitions Elsewhere Can Teach Us About the Prospects for Arab Democracy*. Washington, DC: Brookings Institution Press, 2014. |
| Shadi Hamid | *Temptations of Power: Islamists and Illiberal Democracy in a New Middle East*. New York: Oxford University Press, 2014. |
| Mohamed F. El-Hewie | *Islam Facts and Fiction and the Fight for Egypt*. Seattle, WA: CreateSpace, 2013. |
| Adel Iskandar | *Egypt in Flux: Essays on an Unfinished Revolution*. Cairo, Egypt: American University in Cairo Press, 2013. |

Hazem Kandil       *Soldiers, Spies, and Statesmen: Egypt's Road to Revolt.* Brooklyn, NY: Verso, 2012.

Ashraf Khalil       *Liberation Square: Inside the Egyptian Revolution and the Rebirth of a Nation.* New York: St. Martin's Press, 2012.

Bahgat Korany and Rabab El-Mahdi, eds.       *Arab Spring in Egypt: Revolution and Beyond.* Cairo, Egypt: American University in Cairo Press, 2012.

Tarek Masoud       *Counting Islam: Religion, Class, and Elections in Egypt.* New York: Cambridge University Press, 2014.

Mohamed Fahmy Menza       *Patronage Politics in Egypt: The National Democratic Party and Muslim Brotherhood in Cairo.* New York: Routledge, 2012.

Tamir Moustafa       *The Struggle for Constitutional Power: Law, Politics, and Economic Development in Egypt.* New York: Cambridge University Press, 2009.

Tarek Osman       *Egypt on the Brink: From Nasser to the Muslim Brotherhood.* New Haven, CT: Yale University Press, 2013.

Bruce K. Rutherford       *Egypt After Mubarak: Liberalism, Islam, and Democracy in the Arab World.* Princeton, NJ: Princeton University Press, 2013.

| | |
|---|---|
| Samer Soliman | *The Autumn of Dictatorship: Fiscal Crisis and Political Change in Egypt Under Mubarak*. Stanford, CA: Stanford University Press, 2011. |
| Jeannie Sowers and Chris Toensing, eds. | *The Journey to Tahrir: Revolution, Protest, and Social Change in Egypt*. Brooklyn, NY: Verso, 2012. |
| Joshua Stacher | *Adaptable Autocrats: Regime Power in Egypt and Syria*. Stanford, CA: Stanford University Press, 2012. |
| Carrie Rosefsky Wickham | *The Muslim Brotherhood: Evolution of an Islamist Movement*. Princeton, NJ: Princeton University Press, 2013. |

# Index

# E

# P

CPSIA information can be obtained
at www.ICGtesting.com
Printed in the USA
FFOW05n0048090215

9 780737 772579